Candy Construction

How to Build Edible Race Cars, Castles, and Other Cool Stuff
Out of Store-Bought Candy!

Sharon Bowers

Storey Publishing

The mission of Storey Publishing is to serve our customers by
publishing practical information that encourages
personal independence in harmony with the environment.

Edited by Margaret Sutherland and Franny Shuker-Haines
Art direction and book design by Alethea Morrison
Text production by Liseann Karandisecky

Cover photography by © Kevin Kennefick,
Interior photography by © Kevin Kennfick, except by Mars Vilaubi: pages 10, 26, 60, 86, 108, 124, 144
Food styling by Norma Miller
Set styling by Ann Lewis
Illustrations by © David Sheldon
Diagrams by Missy Shepler
Modeling by Madeline Art, Annabelle Art, and Grace Miller

Storey Publishing
210 MASS MoCA Way
North Adams, MA 01247
www.storey.com

Printed in China by R.R. Donnelley
10 9 8 7 6 5 4 3 2 1

Library of Congress Cataloging-in-Publication Data

Bowers, Sharon.
  Candy construction / by Sharon Bowers.
      p. cm.
  Includes index.
  ISBN 978-1-60342-548-3 (pbk. : alk. paper)
  1. Sugar art. 2. Candy. 3. Confectionery. 4. Cake decorating.
  5. Garnishes (Cookery) I. Title.
TX799.B67 2010
641.8′6—dc22
                        2010020753

For Hugh and Pearse,
the most enthusiastic workers ever to punch a clock
at our Candy Construction Company

Acknowledgments

Sincere thanks to my editor, Margaret Sutherland, for her good advice and deep well of patience — may I never plumb its bottom; to Franny Shuker-Haines for her careful and detailed work on the manuscript; to creative director Alethea Morrison, who continues to astonish me with her talent; to stylists Norma Miller and Ann Lewis and photographer Kevin Kennefick, who created and shot delightful scenes for each project; and to all the wonderful and dedicated team at Storey, including a big smacking kiss for the remarkable Amy Greeman.

Deepest thanks as always to my unflagging friends and colleagues, Jennifer Griffin and Angela Miller.

And most of all, thanks to my dear, funny, and most important, engineering-minded husband, David Bowers. Most of the niftier projects in this book exist thanks to you, and life is fun for the same reason.

CONTENTS

BUILDING PERMITS

BABIES ARE BORN LIKING SWEETNESS, and that natural taste predilection only seems to intensify throughout childhood (and doesn't always disappear in adulthood). No matter how much you may try to avoid giving your kids sugar, there's no way to avoid their passion for it. Like a lot of parents who try to be careful with their kids' sugar intake, I hardly ever gave my first child a cookie till he was two, so eager was I to avoid a sweet tooth. Now, at six, he dreams of running a candy store and adores the movie *Willy Wonka and the Chocolate Factory*. With my second child, I simply shrugged and let him share in whatever loot came my children's way, and he's no more or less obsessed with it than his brother. What's the lesson here? That candy continues to be a big part of childhood. From birthday goodie bags, Valentine and Halloween parties, trips to the general store, and visits to the grandparents, candy is the signal to kids of something festive and special.

And candy *is* fabulously fun. Most children would choose a candy ring or a chocolate bar or a pair of wax lips over a fresh, homemade cookie any day. I'm not so old that I don't remember the thrill myself. As a child, I worshiped candy: the scent, the look, the wrappings, the endless fascinating color and variety — taste was a secondary consideration at best. I spent my first dime ever at a candy store, buying a chewy bar of Bit-O-Honey, and that early transaction remains one of the most fully satisfying purchases I've ever made.

But there has to be a better way to enjoy candy than unlimited consumption. How can a responsible parent let a kid enjoy candy without letting him stuff himself with the junk? The trick is not to *eat* it but to make something *with* it. That's where the projects in this book come in! Kids' eyes light up at a cool and stylish Chocolate Race Car. Their joy is unparalleled when they sport a sassy Arm Candy wristwatch or bracelet. And a whole pyramid, pirate ship, or castle built out of it will be met with oohs and ahs. With a candy construction project, kids can have their candy — and eat a little bit of it, too.

The best part of candy construction is that the fun begins right away for both parent and child. When I was testing and refining the recipes for my first book, *Ghoulish Goodies*, my young sons wouldn't get out of the kitchen. "What are we making next?" they asked continually, which was very gratifying, of course . . . and yet kind of annoying, too. Because, while I was happy to have them participate, and I wanted each recipe to be child-friendly, there were lots of times when I needed to make the cupcakes or the cookies or bake some component before we could start the "fun part" of building and decorating. Before long, I realized that the most consistently enjoyable projects for both parents and kids rarely involved turning on the oven at all. The goodies that were instantly satisfying had ready-made components that let us get straight down to business. And they were the goodies mostly based on store-bought candy.

So I decided to experiment a little. We made a trip to the store for assorted chocolates and candy shapes, mixed up some frosting, and a little bit later: Boom! We had a race car. The resulting confection, complete with a chocolate-bar spoiler, extra-wide cookie wheels that turned on pretzel-stick axels, and a tiny driver in a helmet, was a cross between a Formula One car and Chitty Chitty Bang Bang.

My sons were thrilled — and I had tapped my inner engineer. I started plotting my next move: a fairy-tale castle made from wafer cookies, with battlements, sugar-cone towers, and a drawbridge (my boys are currently into medieval knights, but I found the concept works just as well for girls who like princesses).

"What *can't* we build from candy?" I wondered a few days later, swallowing my pride as I approached the cashier at a drugstore while carrying a basket so laden with chocolates, cookies, and sweets that I felt the need to mutter an embarrassed explanation: "It's for a kids' party." She laughed and said, "Wow, *that* looks like fun."

She was right. Talk about your childhood wishes! Welcome to the Candy Construction Company, where you can even eat the dump trucks.

Really, What About All That Candy?

Like any responsible parent, I try to limit sugar and get plenty of fruits and vegetables into my kids, so what gives with plunking them down at a table full of candy and inviting them to go nuts? When I began designing the projects for this book, I felt very apprehensive as my children hung about my legs whining to help. I was certain they merely wanted to stuff their faces with sweets. So it was with great reluctance that I set them up with a workspace.

To my astonishment, what they did with all that candy was build — really original, creative stuff, too, since they were so inspired by the materials. They took the project at face value: we're building things out of this stuff. The candy became like so much play dough. (And let me hasten to add that I'm not one of those parents who says things like, "No, really, he hates fries but binges on red pepper strips." My kids love candy.) Candy construction is so exciting, however, and so novel to most children, that their primary focus is to create, not eat. And once my kids made their own train or rocket, they were often too proud of their artwork to even consider breaking off parts for a snack. Also, I set a few on-site rules for everyday construction that may work at your house, too.

ON-SITE RULES

1. Absolutely no eating while building. What construction worker snacks on the job?

2. One item can be chosen from among the supplies, or one piece of what was built, but it's to be eaten after cleanup.

3. Candy construction workers always brush their teeth after work.

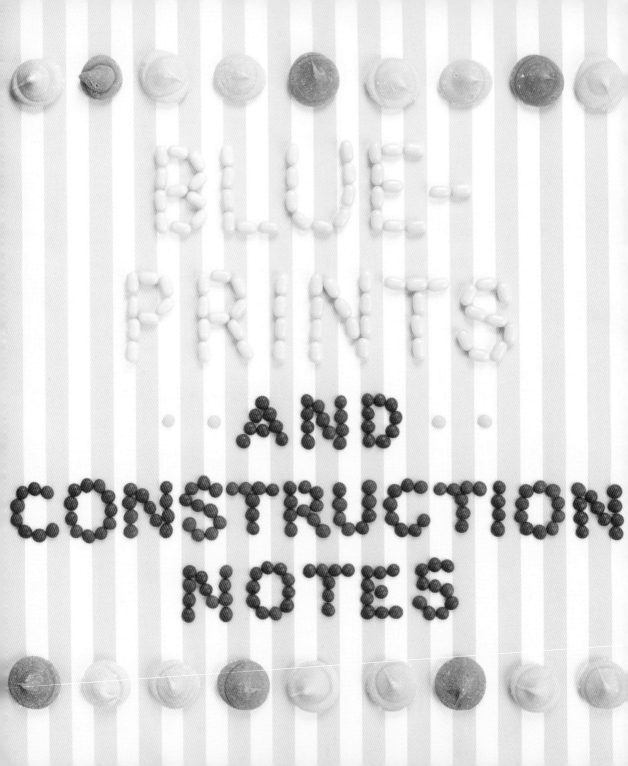

The world of candy is a big place, and things have changed a lot since I was ten. Now there's a much more bedazzling variety of sugary shapes, from rolls and sticks, to ropes and strips, to rings and cubes. You'll find squares and drops of luxury chocolates of all sizes, with different cocoa percentages (and thus different colors), and more cookies and candy bars than you could ever possibly use, much less eat.

There are marshmallows, taffy, and marzipan to shape, cut, and mold, and hard candies in a jewel-like range of colors, shapes, and sizes. And you can buy practically anything in its "gummy" form, from old-fashioned bears and worms, to spiders, sharks, frogs, hippos, turtles, and soda bottles! Finding enough shaped candies to work with is not a problem — selecting among the huge variety of options might be.

Building Supplies

Your best bet for laying in supplies without breaking the bank is to hit the local dollar store. That's the place to find all the candy you need at the best possible prices. And it helps to have a lot of candy when you're building, because you never know when peach-flavored gummy rings or chocolate drops with nonpareils will serve as inspiration. You *can* simply buy the few items you need to complete a project. But the thrill of candy construction is that it extends an open invitation to explore. More often than not, you'll be halfway through a project when you suddenly get a much more exciting idea for how to decorate and personalize your version. For that, you'll want to have a goodly stash of candy in your cupboard.

You'll be glad you shopped at the dollar store, not only because the expense of an inspiring supply drops significantly when everything is a buck, but also because every dollar store carries something different and more exciting than the stuff you'll find at the big-box stores. A Charleston Chew that's 18 inches long? Got it, and for only a dollar. When viewed like any other craft material, candy from the dollar store is much less expensive than buying, say, scrapbook materials. And your kids will be *much* more excited about it.

On-Site Storage

Leftover candy can be used again and again for different projects, so you don't have to worry about the waste of buying a bag of gumdrops when you need only a handful for the item you're currently building. Let's face it: Most candy is made to hang around for a long time. Seal the bags up tightly when you're done. If that's not possible, transfer leftovers to ziplock bags, and keep them in a cool, dry cabinet. Stored this way, most candy will stay fresh, usable, and edible for months.

What's more, each candy-construction project is designed with flexibility in mind. If you can't find sour tape strips, for example, to drape over the hood of your race car, try strips of chewing-gum "tape," which are sold in inch-wide, 6-foot lengths. And if you turn up any unusually shaped or colored candy at a store, perhaps some regional specialty from your area, your inner contractor will soon find a way to put it to good use on your own personal candy-building site.

Mortar and Glue

Even with all this store-bought candy, I'm still a fan of homemade frostings and icings to be used as both glue and coating. (Peanut-butter play dough that's homemade can also be used to form some items, and there's the option to bake your own brownies, if you prefer.) The reason to make your own simple buttercream and royal icing is not because store-bought frosting tastes heavily of chemicals (hardly a persuasive argument when you're eating a "gummy" anything) but because all those emulsifiers and hydrogenated oils make store-bought frosting especially slick and greasy — not at all what you want for sticking things together. Homemade buttercream can vary in thickness depending on the project, and you can color it intensely with paste colors, which have become inexpensive and widely available in the craft section of any big-box store.

Nothing here requires such elaborate frosting piping that you'd need a special bag or piping tips. I remain a big fan of what I think of as "the busy parent's piping bag," better known as a ziplock bag with a tiny hole cut in the corner.

Recipes for basic frosting "mortars" follow, but if you really want to skip all the prep and get right down to the building, you can certainly purchase ready-made frosting. A can of store-bought "buttercream" won't have any butter or cream in it, but it may have a squeeze nozzle that might sometimes be easier to wield than a frosting-laden knife, depending on what you're building. And royal icing often comes in tubes with little nozzles that are just right for decorating tiny items and narrow spaces. If you don't want to blend peanut butter and confectioners' sugar, you can purchase ready-made marzipan and use that for shaping tiny creatures. Whether you buy or make the putty, mortar, and paint at your own job site is your management decision, according to your time and budget!

Vanilla Mortar

This basic buttercream is useful for nearly every project. You can make it thicker by adding less, or no, liquid. Store extra frosting (tightly covered) in the fridge for up to two weeks.

MAKES ABOUT 3 CUPS

What You'll Need

- ½ cup (1 stick) butter, at room temperature
- 4 cups confectioners' sugar (a 1-pound box)
- 1 teaspoon vanilla
- 2–3 tablespoons whole milk or cream

What to Do

Beat the butter with an electric mixer until smooth. Gradually add the sugar, beating until absorbed, then beat in the vanilla. If the frosting is too thick, add the milk or cream, a few teaspoons at a time, until it reaches the consistency you prefer.

Cream Cheese Mortar

Don't use light cream cheese or Neufchâtel: the full-fat kind, slightly chilled, is much denser and has better sticking power. Cream cheese adds a pleasant tang and can help undercut the sweetness in projects that use a lot of frosting. You can substitute this recipe whenever vanilla mortar is called for.

MAKES ABOUT 3 CUPS

What You'll Need

- 1 (3-ounce) package cream cheese, at room temperature
- ¼ cup (½ stick) butter, at room temperature
- 1 teaspoon vanilla
- 4 cups confectioners' sugar (a 1-pound box)

What to Do

With an electric mixer, beat together the cream cheese, butter, and vanilla until fluffy and smooth. Gradually beat in the sugar until fully absorbed and fluffy.

Note for All Mortar Recipes:
For many projects, it helps to begin with a super-thick mortar that you thin out for decorating after the main construction is done.

Milk Chocolate Mortar

This makes a gently flavored, pale chocolate frosting that's even milder if you use Dutch-process cocoa. For sticking power, you may want to make the mortar without any added liquid and stir it in a few teaspoons at a time, if needed.

MAKES ABOUT 3 CUPS

What You'll Need

- ½ cup (1 stick) butter, at room temperature
- 4 cups confectioners' sugar (a 1-pound box)
- 2 tablespoons cocoa powder
- 2–3 tablespoons whole milk or cream

What to Do

Beat the butter with an electric mixer until smooth. Gradually add the sugar and cocoa powder, beating until absorbed. If the frosting is too thick, add the milk or cream, a few teaspoons at a time, until it reaches the consistency you prefer.

Dark Chocolate Mortar

To make a dark chocolate frosting with a silkier texture, replace the cocoa from the milk chocolate icing with melted chocolate chips. Melt them in the microwave on high for one minute, then stir with a fork until smooth. In the unlikely event that the chips still aren't melted, nuke them in 10-second bursts, stirring after each. When chocolate is smooth, let it cool slightly before using.

MAKES ABOUT 3 CUPS

What You'll Need

- ½ cup (1 stick) butter, at room temperature
- 4 cups confectioners' sugar (a 1-pound box)
- ½ cup semisweet chocolate chips, melted and cooled
- 2–3 tablespoons whole milk or cream

What to Do

1. Beat the butter with an electric mixer until smooth. Gradually add the sugar, beating until absorbed.

2. Stir in melted chocolate until well blended. If the frosting is too thick, add the milk or cream, a few teaspoons at a time, until it reaches the consistency you prefer.

Royal Icing Glue

This egg-white-based icing is often used to "flood" cookie surfaces for decorating. It's highly liquid when wet, then dries to a firm, glossy finish. Used sparingly, it makes a great glue that dries hard and strong (well, compared to buttercream), making it the "cement" of candy construction.

MAKES ABOUT 1 CUP

What You'll Need

1 egg white*

1 teaspoon lemon juice

1½ cups confectioners' sugar

* There is a slight risk of Salmonella or other foodborne illness when using raw eggs. If you are concerned, you can use pasteurized egg white or 2 teaspoons of powdered egg white mixed with 2 tablespoons water in place of the raw egg white.

What to Do

1. With a hand mixer, beat the egg white and lemon juice until frothy. With the mixer at medium speed, gradually beat in the confectioners' sugar until the mixture is thick.

2. Turn the mixer to high and beat icing until the mixture is thick and glossy, about 3 minutes. Cover the surface with plastic wrap while waiting to use it.

> **Note:** Royal icing will set to a firm, glossy finish when dry. Extra icing can be stored, tightly covered, in the refrigerator for up to 1 week.

Building Blocks

Many of the projects are constructed around simple, stable structures made of Rice Krispies Treats, brownies, cookies, or other edible "bricks" and pieces. While some of these engineering edibles are easy to find at the store, the classic crisped-rice cubes are better made at home. As for the brownies, you can go either way, but sometimes making them from scratch is worth the effort just for the aroma alone!

Rice Krispies Treats

You'll find variations on this theme in some of the projects, but here's the basic recipe to use as your foundation for designs in this book — and for ones you and your junior engineers dream up yourselves.

What You'll Need

40 large marshmallows

¼ cup (½ stick) butter

6 cups Rice Krispies cereal

What to Do

1. Grease a 9" x 13" pan (or size needed for your project).

2. Melt the marshmallows and butter together in a large saucepan over medium heat, stirring frequently.

3. Stir the Rice Krispies into the marshmallow mixture; pour the mixture into the prepared pan. Smooth the surface and let cool.

Chocolate Variation: To make a chocolate version of Rice Krispies Treats, substitute Cocoa Krispies for the Rice Krispies.

One-Pot Brownies

A tray of these fragrant chocolate goodies may distract your crew, but that's one of the pitfalls (and perks!) of edible architecture.

MAKES 36 (1⅓-INCH) SQUARES

What You'll Need

- ½ cup (1 stick) butter
- ½ cup cocoa
- ¾ cup granulated sugar
- ¾ cup light brown sugar
- 1 teaspoon vanilla
- 4 eggs
- ¾ cup flour
- ½ teaspoon salt

What to Do

1. Preheat oven to 350°F and grease a 9" x 9" baking pan. Cut a square of parchment paper to fit, and line the bottom of the pan.

2. Melt the stick of butter in a large saucepan over medium-low heat, being careful not to let it sizzle or brown. Remove the pan from the heat before the entire stick has melted and whisk in the cocoa; the remaining butter will melt as you stir.

3. Beat in the granulated sugar, brown sugar, and vanilla with a wooden spoon. Add the eggs one at a time, whisking until each is combined before adding the next. When fully combined, add the flour and salt and mix just to combine. Immediately pour the batter into the prepared pan and bake for 17 minutes, until just set.

4. Cool brownies in the pan for 10 minutes, then turn out onto a wire rack and cool.

Peanut-Butter Play Dough

Edible play dough won't feel quite the same as regular, nonedible play dough, but it's a lot more fun to work with. The powdered milk adds body to the peanut butter, and the corn syrup improves the texture. You can substitute honey for corn syrup to make a slightly tastier play dough, but it will be a touch stickier.

MAKES ABOUT 5 CUPS

What You'll Need

- 2 cups creamy peanut butter
- 2 cups confectioners' sugar
- 2 cups powdered milk
- 1¾ cups corn syrup

What to Do

Put the peanut butter, sugar, powdered milk, and corn syrup in a large bowl and mix them together with a wooden spoon until the mixture is too stiff to stir. Then use your hands to mold and knead the play dough into smoothness.

Chocolate Play Dough

You can make a dark and tasty chocolate version of edible play dough by substituting Nutella for the peanut butter. Nutella has a somewhat different texture from peanut butter, so you may need to knead in a bit more corn syrup or powdered sugar to make a workable dough, depending on the humidity of the weather.

MAKES ABOUT 5 CUPS

What You'll Need

- 2 cups Nutella chocolate-and-hazelnut spread
- 2 cups confectioners' sugar
- 2 cups powdered milk
- 1¾ cups corn syrup

What to Do

Put the Nutella, sugar, powdered milk, and corn syrup in a large bowl and mix them together with a wooden spoon until the mixture is too stiff to stir. Then use your hands to mold and knead the play dough into smoothness.

Construction Schedules and Difficulty

These projects are designed so parents can easily build any of them, with or without the children. You may be surprised at how adept little hands are at putting together small pieces of candy, but occasionally there are steps that require the more cautious fingers of a grownup, such as any blueprint that begins "With a sharp paring knife . . ." Or, for example, to get race-car wheels that can actually turn on their pretzel axles, it helps to carefully create a hole in the cookie wheel with a metal skewer. Jobs requiring sharp objects are intended to be performed solely by the senior foreman on the site. In most cases, however, you'll find an easier option for junior workers, such as gluing the wheels on directly with frosting, even if they don't turn.

That's because rigid attention to perfection is highly *discouraged* at the Candy Construction Company. To make every corner square and every edge flat and every wheel spin, you'd need components made of something besides chocolate and sugar. Here, being edible trumps squared-off edges every time. There are no toothpicks, no cotton balls, and no tiny metal parts, which means you can limit your supervision to how *much* they're eating, not *what* they're eating and how safe it is.

And no matter how complex and fancy they look, nearly every project in this book can be built in about an hour — maybe two, at the most, if you're feeling obsessive-compulsive about decorating every inch of your pirate ship. Once all the ingredients and components are assembled, these walls fly up, so to speak, like a building site you pass that seems to be putting up a new floor every day. In fact, it's best if you *don't* stop once you get started. If you lose momentum, your project may end up sitting, half built, like an office building that lost its financing. Press onward, and gloss over any mistakes with a shiny row of jellybeans. It will look fantastic when it's done.

Construction Citations

The Candy Construction Company frowns upon plumb lines and levels. We never let "perfect" crowd out "good enough" or mitigate the sheer pleasure of getting something sweet stuck together!

Preparing Your Building Site

Once the necessary permits are in place, it's time to put down a foundation, and the base you use depends on what you're planning to do with your project. If you're putting the dump truck on top of a birthday cake, for example, you may want to build it on a platter covered by a sheet of waxed paper: that way, the truck won't stick to the work surface before it's transferred to its intended cake top. It helps to have a plate or small cutting board under some of these larger items so you can put them in the fridge or freezer for a few moments, to firm up sticky bits as you're building.

If you're making something smaller, such as little people or race cars, animals or arm candy, you may want to work over a sheet of waxed paper on the counter (for easier cleanup later). These small items make great individual projects for kids to do on rainy days or during play dates. You can also make them yourself and use them to top cupcakes, individual brownies, or even to place into decorative cupcake papers and give out as party favors or special snacks.

Where you need a more stable, perhaps slightly more permanent base is for building larger items such as the Checker Board, Pirate Ship, or Pyramid, where the candy forms just beg to be the centerpiece

of a tableau. If you're not putting these items on top of, for example, a sheet cake (each is just a bit too big for most round layer cakes), then put them on a large cutting board that has been covered smoothly with foil or plastic wrap. Most of the larger projects come with ideas for surrounding the finished masterpiece with appropriate décor. The Pyramid, for example, can sit in the midst of colored-sugar sand with a few candy palm trees around it — even two more pyramids to evoke the scene at Giza. The Pirate Ship can be set afloat in a sea of blue colored sugar, or you can make a fresh batch of icing, color it bright blue, and use a piping bag or a butter knife to make undulating waves all about the boat. You can even tie a jolly boat to the side or out behind the ship for good measure.

If you can't spare your cutting board for a few days, try a large baking sheet, either with or without a rim, and also covered in foil. While it might seem tempting to wrap your base in decorative paper, don't try it if the item is going to sit on the base for longer than about an hour. Nearly any commercial sweet will leach oil or moisture onto the paper and mar the effect of your cheerful wrapping.

Making the Cut

Now and then, you may come across an instruction that sounds nearly impossible, such as "Cut the chocolate wafer cookie in half across the diameter," or "Trim the graham cracker at a 45-degree angle." But even if you think it can't be done, take up your knife and cut — candy is pretty sturdy, even if it seems crumbly or fragile. Trimming candy in a straight line is not a job for the timid. If you try to slowly hack or saw through candy or commercial cookies, the result will likely be crumbling or cracking. When a cut is required, get a large sharp knife, position the item on a cutting board, and cut definitively and boldly in one fell swoop. The straight edge goes to the brave.

Depending on what you're cutting, it may help to chill the item briefly in the fridge or freezer. Rice Krispies Treats, for example, which serve as a sturdy and lightweight base for several of the constructions, stiffen up well when briefly chilled. They can then be cut to size with a chef's knife, or half-sawed, half-sculpted into shape with a serrated bread knife. When working with stickier candy, such as licorice, a pair of scissors may be the easiest tool. In all cases, however, the best tool for cutting is sharp rather than dull. Dull tools require you to use too much force when making a cut, increasing the likelihood of making a mistake or even injuring yourself.

Construction Citations

Our goal is always to maintain an accident-free work site, and any safety violations should be immediately reported to the foreman by younger siblings or friends. The Candy Construction Company has had zero on-the-job accidents and we mean to keep it that way.

Stuck on You

When you're whipping it into a tasty fluff with a mixer, buttercream might not seem especially tacky. Nonetheless, be sure to use a thin layer when sticking parts together. A heavy dollop is much more likely to slide, but a thin layer acts as more of a weld, sticking to the sugary atoms on one side and bonding them firmly to the sugary surface on the other. When you're attaching decorations, such as a row of M&Ms, it's sometimes easier to pipe or spread a narrow strip of icing along the surface, and then push the candy into it, rather than dabbing the back of each candy with frosting and sticking it in place.

Royal icing, made of egg white and sugar, dries hard and firm, not sticky. Thus, it's a good choice for items that kids will likely want to play with and handle rather than just eat, such as the Arm Candy and Race Cars. If the item you're making is just going to sit on top of a cake or cupcake, being sticky won't matter so much, but items children want to touch are better if they're a bit drier.

Candy Construction: Temporary at Best

In 1851, the Crystal Palace served as the center of London's Great Exhibition of the Works of Industry of All Nations. It was an awe-inspiring structure of cast iron and glass, erected in incredible haste for such an impressive building: from initial design to completion, it took less than a year. The Crystal Palace was built

with the intention of being summarily removed after the festivities, although it hung around a bit longer than originally intended.

Think of your candy composition in a similar way. Candy projects are not intended to be kept for long. It may be hard to throw it away when you have put so much effort into it and it's so cute, but the combination of moisture from the frosting mortar and the atmosphere will quickly begin to degrade even the Pyramid in its sugar desert.

If you make your candy project for a festive event, be it a party or a special meal, disposal will occur quickly and naturally. (Even adults can't resist a taste of a fudgy freight train or a Rice Krispies ship.) If you've made it just for fun and you find it taking up counter space in your kitchen after a while, the best thing you can do with your candy project is let the kids and other interested parties have a taste while it's still fresh enough to eat — and then throw the rest away. Letting a candy project sit until it falls apart (or, worse, is invaded by insect life!) is a violation of all Fun Rules put in place by the project management.

Sometimes you may need to store a project for a few days. In that case, the refrigerator is the safest place, preventing atmospheric humidity and warmth from causing pieces to topple, and keeping out bugs. Cold may cause chocolate to "bloom" (meaning spots of white cocoa butter will start to appear on the surface), but returning it to room temperature will generally remove the bloom. Be aware that humidity in the refrigerator will also soften sugary items such as Rice Krispies Treats, so balance whether you're more worried about melting your chocolate and buttercream or ruining the texture of your Treats. In or out of the fridge, wrap the candy loosely in plastic wrap or in a large plastic bag, and don't keep it in the fridge longer than about four days.

THINGS THAT GO VROOM

Anyone who has walked past a building site with a child knows that kids love to watch big machines doing their thing. The younger set seems to be endlessly fascinated with things that construct, wreck, fly, and go fast. So, why not combine children's natural engineering enthusiasms with their innate candy-loving inclinations? On your mark, get set, and go build yourselves a dump truck, crane or train, race car or helicopter, or even a missile to Mars!

CANDY
CONSTRUCTION SITE

The workers are working . . . the walls are starting to rise . . . the project is getting built, and it's right on schedule! Yes, the Candy Construction Site is the place where childhood dreams come true, ideal for little ones obsessed with dump trunks, cranes, and construction workers. A lightweight Rice Krispies Treat base means this crane probably won't meet safety standards, but the candy boom won't let you hoist anything dangerously heavy anyway.

On top of a cake, either the crane or the dump truck will shine. But as a stand-alone building site, it's hard not to let your imagination run away with you. Set both pieces of equipment on crushed chocolate cookie "dirt." Build half a wall out of any type of hard-candy rocks, stuck together with frosting mortar. Make piles of building materials from a mound of chopped-jelly-bean rubble, to a pile of graham-cracker lumber, to a neat stack of bricks made from individual squares of a chocolate bar. Note that the measurements are approximations; you don't need to measure to make it work.

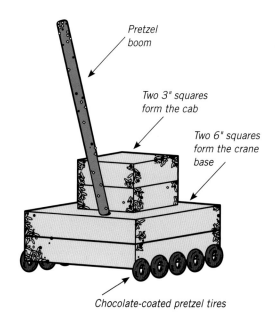

The CRANE

What You'll Need

* Vanilla Mortar (see page 14) or 1 can store-bought white frosting
* Yellow paste coloring
* Rice Krispies Treats (see page 17)
* Licorice strings or red decorating gel
* Dots, gumdrops, or M&Ms
* Chocolate Mortar (see page 15), either milk or dark, or a tube of black or brown decorating gel
* 10 mini chocolate-coated pretzel rounds (the ones in the 100-calorie snack packs are just right) or Mini Oreos
* 1 pretzel rod
* Bubble-gum tape, optional
* Graham-cracker squares, optional

What to Do

1. Color the Vanilla Mortar bright yellow with a few dabs of the food coloring.

2. From the cooled 9" × 13" pan of Rice Krispies Treats, cut two 6" squares and glue one on top of the other with mortar. From the remaining 3" × 13" strip, cut two 3" × 3" pieces and glue them together, one on top of the other. Center the 3" squares on top of the 6" squares and attach with mortar.

Pretzel boom

Two 3" squares form the cab

Two 6" squares form the crane base

Chocolate-coated pretzel tires

3. Frost the entire crane with yellow mortar.

4. Use trimmed lengths of licorice string to outline the windows on either side of the cab and a door on one side. (You can also use decorating gel to pipe on the windows and door.) Glue Dots, gumdrops, or M&Ms around the top or at the four corners of the roof.

5. To make tires, use Chocolate Mortar to attach five mini chocolate-coated pretzel rounds to either side of the base of the crane. If you like, run a tread around them by wrapping them in a long strip of bubble-gum tape.

6. To make the boom:
  ⊙ Use a serrated knife to cut a small notch at the top of a pretzel rod. Push the end of a licorice string into the notch; you won't need a deep groove to hold the licorice securely.
  ⊙ Use the tip of a knife or skewer to make a small hole in the top of the 6" square, next to the cab. Push the pretzel rod boom into the hole, twisting it into the Rice Krispies Treats until it stands firmly in place.
  ⊙ If you like, you can tie a pretzel tire to the end of the licorice rope. Load a flat square shape with gumdrops or other candy, so the crane has a load to lift. A stack of graham cracker squares makes a good pallet.

> **Easy Variation:** Use a longer piece of licorice string and glue it with mortar to the cab side of the boom, draping it over the top so that it falls down along the other side.

7. If you like, decorate the outside of the crane with rows of Dots, gumdrops, and/or M&Ms.

The DUMP TRUCK

What You'll Need

* Vanilla Mortar (see page 14) or 1 can store-bought white frosting
* Yellow paste coloring
* Rice Krispies Treats, plain or chocolate variation (see page 17)
* Dark Chocolate Mortar (see page 15) or a tube of black or brown decorating gel
* 2 graham crackers

* 6 regular-size Oreos
* 3 Nutter Butter Bites or Oreos Golden Mini Bites
* Licorice strings or red decorating gel
* Dots, gumdrops, M&Ms, or other small round candy
* 3 regular-size Oreos, crushed in a ziplock bag with a rolling pin or wooden spoon
* Pretzel rod, optional
* Half-gallon block ice cream or 2 frozen pound cakes, optional

What to Do

1. Color the Vanilla Mortar bright yellow with a few dabs of the food coloring.

2. From the cooled 9" × 13" pan of Rice Krispies Treats, cut a 2" × 7" rectangle for the chassis. Then cut a 3" × 7" rectangle for the truck body. Glue the pieces together with vanilla mortar, centering the smaller piece underneath the larger one.

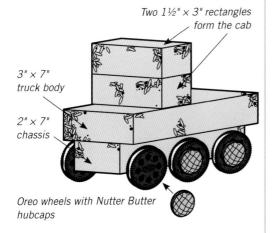

Two 1½" × 3" rectangles form the cab

3" × 7" truck body

2" × 7" chassis

Oreo wheels with Nutter Butter hubcaps

3. To form the cab, cut two more rectangles from the rice mixture, each about 1½" × 3". Stack and glue them together with mortar and then glue the cab onto the truck base, 1½" from one end. Frost the cab and truck base yellow. Slather extra frosting in front of the cab to form a rounded hood.

4. To make the bucket (back of the truck):

- ⊙ Break the graham crackers into four squares. Place a graham-cracker square on your work surface. This will be the base of the bucket.
- ⊙ Arrange the remaining graham-cracker rectangles around the base to form the sides and back of the bucket, using chocolate mortar to hold it all together. The side pieces should sit *on top* of the base; the back should butt up *next to* it.
- ⊙ Set the bucket in the fridge for 10 minutes to harden the mortar, if necessary. Attach the bucket with mortar to the flat bed of the truck.

> **Fun Variation:** Instead of gluing the bucket down flat, use a piece of pretzel rod to prop it up, like a hydraulic lift, as if the bucket were dumping. Use dabs of icing to secure.

5. To make black-tire wheels with hubcaps:

- ⊙ Lay out the six regular-size Oreos.
- ⊙ Split the Nutter Butter Bites in two, dab mortar on the back, and press one in the center of each Oreo.
- ⊙ Dab mortar on the other side of the Oreos and stick them to the sides of the truck's chassis. The cookies will help raise the truck off the ground, with their top edge supporting the body. It helps to

have someone hold up the truck body while you press the cookies in place.

⊙ Set the whole truck in the refrigerator for 10 minutes to firm up the cookies, if needed.

6. For the finishing touches:

⊙ Use trimmed lengths of licorice string to outline the windows on either side of the cab and the windshield. (You can use decorating gel to pipe on the windows.)

⊙ Use Dots, gumdrops, and/or M&Ms to make headlights and taillights on the truck. Add safety lights or reflectors on top of the cab and along the sides, as you like.

⊙ Fill the bucket with crushed-Oreo dirt and sprinkle with M&Ms or gumdrops or any other candy for texture.

> **Fun Variation:** You can also make the dump truck base with slabs of ice cream from a hard-frozen half-gallon block or with two slightly frozen pound cakes.

CANDY CONSTRUCTION WORKERS

What You'll Need

* Malted milk balls or candy raspberries (such as Haribo, see page 44)
* Gumdrops
* Vanilla Mortar (use leftovers from the Crane or Dump Truck)
* Soft-eating black and red licorice, Twizzlers, or any other licorice stick (the soft style is more pliable)
* Pretzel sticks
* Banana shapes from miniature fruit candy (such as Runts)
* Licorice Allsorts, optional
* Jelly beans, optional

What to Do

1. To make each construction worker's head, use a sharp paring knife to cut off the top quarter of a malted milk ball or a candy raspberry. Discard the top. For the helmet, slice a gumdrop or a malted milk ball in half and use mortar to attach one half to the top of the candy head.

2. To make the torso, use a dab of mortar to attach a gumdrop to the construction worker's head.

> **Fun Variation:** Use layered Licorice Allsorts for the torsos. The colorful layers will create "striped" shirts for your construction workers. Trim the square shapes with a small knife or leave them blocky.

3. To make the arms, cut ¾" pieces of soft-eating licorice and attach them with mortar to the worker's torso. Or use a short length of pretzel stick as a sort of toothpick, sticking one end into the licorice and the other into the gumdrop body.

4. To make the legs, cut two pieces of red or black soft-eating licorice about 1½" long. Roll and shape the legs into even rounds (this licorice is very pliable). If you like, glue jelly beans on the end of the licorice for the feet.

5. Attach the legs to the base of the torso with a bit of mortar. Snip the arms a bit shorter if your person looks disproportionate.

6. Make tools for the workers:
- To make a shovel, flatten and shape a piece of the soft licorice into a shovel head, stick half of a pretzel stick into it for a handle, and prop it against a worker.
- For a jackhammer, take another pretzel stick and use mortar to glue a crosspiece (made from a quarter-length of a pretzel stick) to the top; lean it against the front of a worker.
- To make a pickaxe or hammer, glue a tiny banana fruit shape to the end of a half-pretzel stick.

FUDGE BROWNIE
STEAM TRAIN

A box of store-bought brownies, such as Little Debbie Fudge Brownies, serves as the super-easy base for a charming chocolate choo-choo. You can make your train a midnight express by using all chocolate components, or brighten it up with lots of colorful candy decorations and vivid wheels. It's a great cake topper, arranged in a circle on top of a round layer cake, or shooting straight across the plains of a sheet cake. It's also fun to display on a covered cutting board or baking sheet, perhaps amid chocolate-cookie rubble for dirt and set atop some frosting or licorice tracks.

The packaged brownies and Swiss rolls tend to be sticky enough that you don't need much frosting to hold your train together. But since you will still need a few teaspoons to attach the chocolate-bar pieces to the tender and boxcar, this is a great time to use store-bought frosting. You will also need two packaged Swiss rolls or Twinkies to get the barrel shape of the steam engine's body and the tanker car.

MAKES ONE 5-CAR FREIGHT TRAIN, ABOUT 18″ LONG

What You'll Need

* 1 (13-ounce) box fudge brownies (such as Little Debbie, which has two 2" brownie squares to a package)
* 1 package "Swiss Rolls" (such as Little Debbie or Hostess Ho Hos)
* Chocolate Mortar (see page 15) or 1 can store-bought chocolate frosting
* 1 length soft-eating licorice
* M&Ms or jelly beans

* 28 hard round candies (such as butterscotch or peppermint) or mini sandwich cookies (such as Nutter Butter Bites or Mini Oreos)
* 2 (1.55-ounce) chocolate bars, such as Hershey's (the kind that are evenly divided into rectangles)
* 2 regular-size Oreos
* 1 piece of red strip candy, such as Sour Strips or Sour Power Belts (you can also use strip bubble gum if can't find Sour Strips)
* 1 fun-size Snickers bar
* Butterscotch hard candies or additional peppermints, optional

The ENGINE

What to Do

1. To make the base (the same for all cars, with a slight variation for the tender):

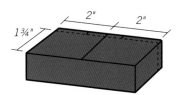

Cut a ¼" strip off the long side of two attached brownies.

- From a 2-pack rectangle of brownies, cut a ¼" strip off the long side of the rectangle, leaving a rectangle about 1¾" × 4". Trim about ¼" off the short side of this rectangle. This isn't strictly necessary but it helps the final steam engine look like it's in proportion. The train base is now 1¾" × 3¾".
- Cut the long trimmed-off ¼" piece into three equal strips and place them beneath the large rectangle as shown to

make the wheel supports. Don't worry about using mortar at this point: the brownies are sticky enough that they'll hold together without it.

Cut the ¼" strip into three pieces and press them against the bottom of the brownie.

2. To make the front of the engine, cut off and discard about 1" from the front of a Swiss roll. Place the remaining piece on the top of the brownie, with the cut end flush to the front edge and facing outward.

3. To make the cab and roof:
- Take a fresh pack of brownies and again trim a ¼" strip off the long side. The brownie rectangle will have a mark down the middle where it can divide easily into two squares. Cut along this line, then take one of the resulting halves and slice it in two.
- Stand these two rectangles on end behind the Swiss roll to form the cab of the engine.
- Lay the remaining square on top of the cab to make the roof.

Cut a ½" piece of soft-eating licorice and set it on top of the Swiss roll to make the spout, or funnel. (If you don't have round rolls of soft, moldable licorice, use a small piece of brownie and roll it between your fingers to shape a cylinder.) Balance an M&M or jelly bean on top.

4. To make the wheels:
- Unwrap six round hard candies. Use frosting to glue them to the supports on both sides of the engine. For a holiday train, use red-and-white peppermints.
- For an all-chocolate train, use mini chocolate sandwich cookies, or substitute mini golden sandwich cookies.

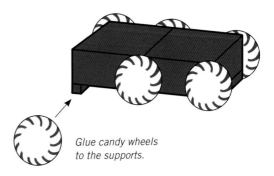

Glue candy wheels to the supports.

The TENDER

What to Do

1. To make the base:
   - From a 2-pack rectangle of brownies, cut a ¼" strip off the long side of the rectangle, as you did for the engine. This time, separate the two-brownie square along the dividing line and discard one half.
   - Cut the trimmed-off ¼" strip into two supports and place them under the remaining rectangle as shown.
   - Put the tender base behind the engine on your base or cake top.

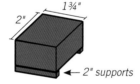

Rectangular tender with two wheel supports

2. Unwrap four pieces of round hard candy or select four mini sandwich cookies for wheels. Use frosting to glue them to the wheel supports on both sides of the tender.

3. To form an open box on top of the tender base (to fill with cookie coal), break off four pieces of the chocolate bar. Gently press the long edges of the chocolate-bar pieces into the brownie base (you may need a little dab of frosting to help them stick).

Candy-bar coal box

4. To make coal for the tender, put the two regular-size Oreos in a ziplock bag and, using a rolling pin, roll them into coarse crumbs. Spoon this coal into the tender. Save leftovers for the open boxcar.

The TANKER CAR

What to Do

1. From a fresh pack of brownies, make a base in the same way as for the engine (step 1).

2. Set the tanker car base in place behind the tender. Unwrap six pieces of round hard candy or select six mini sandwich cookies for wheels. Use frosting to glue them to the wheel supports on both sides of the tanker.

3. Put a Swiss roll on top to make the tanker. For the cap, place an M&M atop a short piece of licorice or a bit of brownie rolled into a flat cylinder.

The OPEN BOXCAR

What to Do

1. From a fresh pack of brownies, make a base in the same way as for the engine (step 1).

2. Set the boxcar base in place behind the tanker. Unwrap six pieces of round hard candy or select six mini sandwich cookies for wheels. Use frosting to glue them to the wheel supports on both sides of the boxcar.

3. Break a chocolate bar into two long adjoining rectangles of two pieces each, joined at the short end, and two single rectangles. To make the open box, use a bit of frosting to stick the long rectangles to the long sides of the base and the short rectangles along the ends.

4. Fill the open boxcar with the remaining chocolate-cookie rubble from the tender, and scatter the top with colorful M&Ms or jelly beans. You can also fill the boxcar with crushed hard candies, such as a stack of gold nuggets made from butterscotch, or a delivery from the North Pole made from a stack of crushed peppermints.

The CABOOSE

What to Do

1. From a fresh pack of brownies, make a base in the same way as for the engine (step 1).

2. Set the caboose base in place behind the open boxcar. To make the wheels, unwrap six pieces of round hard candy or select six mini sandwich cookies. Use frosting to glue them to the wheel supports on both sides of the caboose.

3. To make the car:
   - From a fresh pack of brownies cut two ¾" × 2½" pieces.
   - Set them on their sides on the middle of the caboose base to make a block (similar to the cab of the engine).
   - To make the caboose red, wrap a piece of red Sour Strip, about 8" long, around the outer edges of this central piece.

4. To make the roof and cupola:
   - With a sharp knife, cut the sides off the Snickers bar, about ½" from the edge. This piece will be the curved roof of the caboose. Use frosting to stick the piece to the top of the caboose, curved side up.
   - Trim a short piece of licorice or roll a soft piece of brownie into a cylinder. Glue this to the top center of the curved roof and top with an M&M.

RACE CARS

If you want to top a birthday cake to impress a race-car lover, the more complex Formula One design is definitely the way to go. If you want little race cars to dress up the tops of cupcakes, or to let your kids make a track-full, the mini toy cars are for you.

If you want your wheels to really roll, you can stick them to the body of the car with toothpicks, but I seriously don't recommend that for kids. When I first went to eat a chocolate race car (hey, it was late at night and I could hear that Snickers bar calling from its garage in my freezer!), I accidentally bit into the tip of a toothpick that had broken off in the frozen confection. Fortunately, I was eating the prototype; my boys had made their cars with pretzel sticks.

The gumdrops that make the car's tiny driver are widely available in the candy section of Toys"R"Us stores nationwide. Look for the Haribo brand. Shaped just like real raspberries or blackberries, the individual seeds of each berry are clearly delineated, which lets you pry out two seeds from the red berry and replace them with two from the black, to make bright and beady little eyes for your speed racer.

▼FORMULA ONE ◄CAR

What You'll Need

* 8 regular-size or Double Stuf Oreos
* Royal Icing Glue (see page 16)
* 1 king-size Snickers or other large chocolate-covered candy bar
* 1 Reese's Peanut Butter Cup
* 1 Hershey's Miniatures bar (or other small chocolate bar)
* 1 (1.55-ounce) chocolate bar, such as Hershey's (the kind that is evenly divided into rectangles)
* 1 red candy raspberry (such as Haribo)
* 1 black candy blackberry (such as Haribo)
* 4 small pretzel sticks
* Sour candy strips in red or green, at least 8" long
* Multicolored sour candy strips, optional

What to Do:

1. To make four wheels of double thickness, lay out four Oreos. Slather the top of each with royal icing, and then cover with another Oreo. Set aside to dry slightly.

2. To make the auto body, put the king-size candy bar, right-side up, on a nonstick work surface (such as a plate or a small cutting board). Use a sharp paring knife to fashion a cockpit for the driver: trim out a shallow U-shape about three-quarters from one end of the candy bar where the seat will go.

3. To make a hole for the axles, use the tip of the knife (or a metal or bamboo skewer) to "drill" two holes all the way through the candy bar about ¾" from the front end and about ¾" from the back end. These are where you'll insert the pretzel-stick axles. (You may need to wiggle the skewer in the hole a little bit to make sure it's big enough for the pretzel sticks to fit through.)

4. To make the seat and seat back, slice the Reese's cup in half to make two semicircles. Use royal icing to glue one, bottom-side down, in the cockpit. Glue the other half with the cut side down, making a semicircular seat back behind where the driver will sit.

5. To make the front grill, glue the miniature chocolate bar (at an angle, *see photo*) to the front end of the car with royal icing.

6. To make the rear spoiler, break off a 3-section piece of the large chocolate bar and position it above the Reese's cup. You'll need a good dollop of royal icing to make it stick.

7. To make the tires, carefully and gently "drill" a hole through the center of each Oreo tire with a skewer. Work gently so that the cookie doesn't break; your hole should go only through the top cookie and into the filling. (You might need to wiggle the skewer to make the hole big enough for a pretzel stick to fit through.)

8. To make the driver:
- Slice off the top third of one black and one red gumdrop berry. Place the black top onto the red berry. (You may need a little icing to make it stick if the candy is not moist.)
- For the eyes, pry out two red seeds from the face of the red berry, and replace it with two black seeds from the black berry. (You can make a mouth and nose if you like, but your little driver's face may get a bit crowded.) Place the driver in the cockpit, using a little icing to hold him in place.

9. To attach the wheels, carefully insert the pretzel rods into the sides of the candy bar, and then carefully fit an Oreo wheel onto each rod. If the holes are just large enough, the wheels will actually turn!

10. Paint the auto body by draping strips of sour candy over the hood, starting just in front of the driver and stopping just behind the grill. Trim the strips to fit and stick them down with a bit of icing.

> **Fun Variation:** Use contrasting strips of sour candy for racing stripes.

TOY CAR

What You'll Need

* Miniature Snickers or other miniature chunky candy bar
* Royal Icing Glue (see page 16)
* 4 mini sandwich cookies, such as Mini Oreos
* 1 mini Tootsie Roll
* 1 peanut M&M
* Strip candy, such as Sour Strips or Sour Power Belts (you can also use strip bubble gum if can't find Sour Strips)
* Red decorating gel, optional

What to Do

1. To make the body of the car:
   ⊙ Use a sharp paring knife to carve a U-shaped curve out of the top of the candy bar for a cockpit.
   ⊙ Glue four mini-sandwich-cookie wheels onto the sides with royal icing.
   ⊙ Glue a mini Tootsie Roll across the back behind the cockpit.
   ⊙ If you like, cover the white filling of the cookie tires with decorating gel.

2. To make the driver, dab a bit of icing on the tip of a peanut M&M and push it into the cockpit.

3. Drape a slice of sour strip across the front to make a hood, using a thin slick of icing to glue it down. If you like, cut a narrow strip of a different color and add a contrasting racing stripe down the middle.

BIPLANE AND HELICOPTER

Candy airplane designs abound, but they tend to involve packages of gum tied with yarn or rubber bands to a roll of SweeTarts, or wrapped candies stuck together with glue guns. A plane that's entirely edible is a much more exciting item for kids, and it's also easier for them to build. If you can't find wafer cookies long enough to be your wings, use two cookies, as shown in the photograph.

The helicopter might need an adult to help build the rotor, but that adult needs only a sharp knife and a steady hand, so don't be intimidated. However, if you'd like a slightly simpler version, simply crisscross two strips of regular, old-fashioned chewing gum, preferably a stick of Doublemint that's been sitting around unwrapped for a while. When it dries out slightly, it's stiff enough to fly, or at least to serve as a rotor!

CHOCOLATE BIPLANE

What You'll Need

* 1 Charleston Chew
* M&Ms
* Chocolate Mortar (see page 15) or 1 can store-bought chocolate frosting
* 5 filled chocolate wafer cookies
* 3 Mini Oreos
* Pretzel sticks
* 1 (1.55 ounce) chocolate bar, such as Hershey's (the kind that is evenly divided into rectangles)

Blueprints

Charleston Chews are about a foot and a half long. They make terrific biplane bodies, but if you can't find Charleston Chews, try using a stick from a Twix or a Kit-Kat bar.

What to Do

1. To make the body of the plane, cut off a 4" piece of Charleston Chew. On the underside of the candy bar, make a narrow groove at the back end. Slip in an M&M to serve as the rear wheel, using a drop of mortar to affix if necessary.

2. To make the bottom wing, use mortar to attach two wafer cookies end to end and to the underside of the plane's body, about ½" from the nose of the plane.

3. To make the axle, cut a ½" slice off the tip of another wafer cookie. Flip the plane over, and center this piece across the underside of the plane, behind the bottom wing; mortar in place. For wheels, mortar a Mini Oreo to either side of this central axle and to the sides of the plane.

4. Flip the plane over (it should now balance on the wheels). To make the top wing, use mortar to attach two wafer cookies end to end and use more mortar to attach this wing to the top of the plane, directly over the bottom wing. For greater stability, break off two short pretzel stick pieces and push them gently into the wafer surfaces between the wings, as shown.

5. To make the engine, use a bit of mortar to stick a Mini Oreo on the nose of the plane. For the propeller, take another wafer cookie and pull a wafer layer off the filling. Cut two pieces from the long side of this thin wafer layer, each about ⅛" wide and about 1" long, and attach them in a cross on the front of the Oreo engine with mortar.

6. To make the tail:
   ⊙ Break a two-rectangle piece off the end of the Hershey bar, keeping them attached to one another at the narrow ends.
   ⊙ Break off a third rectangle from the Hershey bar and trim about a third of it away. Use mortar to fasten this shortened piece upright onto the central seam of the two joined pieces. With more mortar, attach this tailpiece onto the tail of the plane, just above the M&M rear wheel.

VANILLA HELICOPTER

What You'll Need

* 2 Golden Oreos
* Vanilla Mortar (see page 14) or 1 can store-bought white frosting
* Blue fruit leather
* 2 pretzel sticks
* 1 pack Golden Oreo Fun Stix, or any cigar-shaped cookie
* 2 filled vanilla wafer cookies

What to Do

1. To make the helicopter's body:
   - Remove the cookie top from an Oreo and use a knife to cut it in half. Cut a small rectangle off one of the straight edges to make a gap that will anchor the copter's tail.

Cut a small rectangle off the straight edge of the halved cookie top.

- Fit the cookie halves back together, pressing them back onto the filling. There will now be a small channel along the center line of the cut top cookie.
- Use mortar to stick the cookie to a second Oreo, with the little channel on the inside.
- Cut a square of fruit leather and glue it to the front of the cookies to serve as the windshield.

2. To make the helicopter's tail (or boom), insert a pretzel stick into the little channel that you've carved inside the helicopter body. The pretzel should fit firmly (you probably won't need any additional mortar to stick it down). Don't worry if the pretzel seems too short for your helicopter: you'll be extending the boom later.

3. To make the helicopter's skids:
   - Unwrap a set of Fun Stix (they come two to a foil pack). Cut one of the stix in half to make two 1½" pieces.
   - Use mortar to attach the two pieces side by side. Position them beneath the cookie body *(see photo)*, with the tail/boom tipped up at a slight angle, and glue them in place with the mortar.
   - Break off a small piece of a pretzel stick and glue it on top of the landing skids, wedged behind the round Oreo body.

This gives the helicopter stability and keeps the body from rolling back.

4. To finish the tail, trim the remaining Fun Stix to about 2". Slide it down onto the pretzel. The icing inside the Fun Stix will hold the pieces together.

5. To make the main rotor:
    ◉ Take a wafer cookie and separate the top wafer from the rest of the cookie (some of the filling may come off with it).

With a sharp chef's knife, cut this piece lengthwise to make two strips ¼" wide.
    ◉ Stick the strips together in an X with a bit of mortar.
    ◉ Attach the rotor to the top of the cookie body with mortar.

6. To make the rear rotor, repeat the steps for making the main rotor, but trim the wafer pieces even narrower, into ⅛" strips, and shorten them to about ¾" long. Attach it to the end of the boom with a dab of mortar.

OUTER SPACE

The curvy lines of this fat little rocket make it look just like a cartoon ship. You can help plump up your rocket's outlines by pouring the Rice Krispies Treats (see page 17) that form the core into a small loaf pan, resulting in a short, thick shape. Grease or butter the loaf pan well before scraping in the mixture; you may want to line the pan with parchment and butter it, too. Cool completely and turn out the entire loaf, compressing it gently with your hands before you start to carve. Use a serrated knife to saw and shape, removing everything that doesn't look like a rocket. The mini missiles (page 58) are much more businesslike — if you can call anything businesslike that features a Kiss for the cone!

The SPACESHIP

What You'll Need

* Rice Krispies Treats recipe (see page 17), but follow pouring instructions below
* 2 graham crackers
* Vanilla Mortar (see page 14) or 1 can store-bought white frosting
* Blue paste food coloring
* 7 mini chocolate-coated pretzel rounds (the ones in the 100-calorie snack packs are just right)
* Dots or M&Ms
* Red Hots or Nerds, or another small, round candy
* Hershey's Kisses or cotton candy, red or orange
* Blue fruit leather, optional

What to Do

1. Butter an 8" × 4" loaf pan. Pour the Rice Krispies mixture into the loaf pan while still warm and press it down with your buttered hands to compact it. Allow it to cool and become firm, 20 to 30 minutes, and then turn the cooled rice mixture out of the loaf pan.

Blueprints

If you want an even brighter rocket, add orange or blue paste food coloring to the melted marshmallow mixture when you make the Rice Krispies Treats. Start with a little, and add a little bit more, stirring well each time, until you have the shade you want. Remember that when you stir in the cereal, the color will lighten a bit, but not much, so the shade of the marshmallow mixture should be about as intense as you'd like the final product to be. Once you've added the cereal, if you don't find the shade intense enough, don't try to repair it: the color won't distribute evenly once the cereal has been added. Just make a note to yourself for next time. For now, you can compensate by making your decorations even brighter!

2. To make the body, use a stiff serrated knife (not a thin-bladed, flexible one, which won't shape the material well) to trim the loaf into a rough football shape. Make it narrow and pointed at the top. Slice the bottom end flat, and then cut three vertical grooves about 3" long and ¼" deep, equidistant around the base of the rocket.

Trim Rice Krispies Treats into a football shape with a flat bottom.

Cut three vertical grooves into the base for tailfins.

3. To make the tailfins, use a sharp paring knife to cut three whole graham crackers into roughly triangular shapes. Round off the sides a bit to resemble a shark fin. Once you cut the first cracker to your satisfaction, you can use it as a template so the others are about the same size.

Construction Citations

When cutting graham crackers, score the surface first in the shape you want to cut. Scoring lightly with a sharp chef's knife helps prevent breakage when you make the actual cut through the cracker. A serrated knife may seem tempting because you can saw gently through the cracker, but you'll likely get less breakage by making one short, determined cut over the scoring.

4. Color 1 cup of vanilla mortar blue with a few dabs of food coloring. Put the mortar in a ziplock bag and cut off one corner to make a piping bag.

5. To make the portholes:
   ⊙ Using the tip of a paring knife, cut three shallow circles into the rocket. They should be the size of the chocolate-covered pretzel rings. Scrape the Rice Krispies out of each circle so you can set the chocolate-covered pretzel rings in flush. Dab some mortar on the back of a pretzel ring and press into place.

• Fill in the center of each porthole with blue frosting, and, if you like, press in a Dot or M&M.

> **Easy Variation:** Glue the portholes onto the surface of the spaceship with blue mortar as seen in the photograph on page 55. Fill with blue mortar or small rounds of blue fruit leather.

6. Lay the rocket on its side. Pipe a thin line of blue frosting into the grooves around the rocket base and stick in the fins. Put the rocket in the fridge, still on its side, to firm it up, 10 to 15 minutes.

7. Continue working with the rocket on its side. Glue small round candies, such as Red Hots, into the spaceship to make rivets. If you like, pipe a line of blue frosting to outline a door. Add a dot of frosting for a doorknob, pressing a small round candy into it to complete the effect.

8. Set the rocket upright, on a plate or on a cake, and put a pile of silver Hershey's Kisses or a plume of red or orange cotton candy beneath it to simulate the smoke and fire of takeoff.

HEAT-SEEKING MINI-MISSILES

What You'll Need
* Oreo Fun Stix or any cigar-shaped cookie
* Chocolate Oreos
* Chocolate or Vanilla Mortar (see page 14) or 1 can store-bought frosting
* Hershey's Kisses (one per rocket)
* Caramel Cow Tales, optional

What to Do
1. Make the body of each missile from an Oreo Fun Stix. Keep the Fun Stix long for a tall missile or trim them down for a shorter one (but don't cut them so short that the nosecone is out of proportion).

> **Fun Variation:** Your favorite cylindrical cookie makes a great missile, but you can also try using a caramel Cow Tale for a true candy flavor.

2. Separate the Oreos. Stand each missile in a cookie half with frosting.

3. To make the fins, use a sharp chef's knife to cut the unfrosted cookie halves into triangles with two straight edges. The rounded edge of the cookie will curve down from the missile body. To glue them in place, dip the straight edges of each fin in frosting and press it into the cookie filling against the bottom of the Fun Stix. You will need three fins per missile.

4. Unwrap a Kiss and put a dollop of frosting on its base, and then glue it to the top of the missile.

Blueprints

Not in the market for a big rocket? Try a little missile, cut to size, either for kids to make for fun, or to use as cupcake decoration. If you're putting your big rocket on a cake as a topper, try pressing attendant mini missiles around the sides of the cake.

Tap into your child's spirit of adventure with some far-flung, fanciful projects! Whether your young ones dream of Egyptian exploration or navigating a pirate ship to Neverland, they can get halfway there with these dazzling displays of sweet treats. And who can resist creating their own outer-space aliens out of gooey goodies? Or making the ultimate Fairy-Tale castle, complete with draw-bridge — and completely edible? The most important ingredient in these projects: Imagination!

PYRAMIDS
OF GIZA

If you're looking for an educational engineering project, you can build architecturally correct pyramids out of sugar cubes — a painstaking, laborious, well, *job* that brings to mind what all those Egyptian slaves must have suffered thousands of years ago, but without the heavy lifting. If you're looking for a really cool candy pyramid project, however, you've come to the right desert. Or dessert. This party-time pyramid is roughly shaped with graham-cracker bricks and icing mortar and faced with vanilla wafer gravel. It also holds a secret worth excavating. Sure, you *could* skip the surprise marshmallow-and-chocolate interior, but it does make for a delightful sort of pyramidal s'more.

Make the Great Pyramid and set it amidst blowing sands of sugar, surrounded with a gumdrop palm tree or two, or make three pyramids, each slightly smaller than the other, and line them up for the real Giza effect. No back-breaking labor here — they're surprisingly fast to build once your materials are in place. For inspiration, it's fun to check out www.pyramidcam.com for a live feed from a camera trained day and night on the Pyramids of Giza.

The PYRAMID

MAKES 1 PYRAMID

What You'll Need

* Half of 1 (14-ounce) box of graham crackers
* 2 (1.55-ounce) chocolate bars
* Vanilla Mortar (see page 14) or 1 can store-bought white frosting
* 1 (7-ounce) jar Marshmallow Fluff
* 2 cups vanilla wafers
* 2 cups granulated sugar
* Liquid food coloring, orange (or yellow and red to make orange)
* Shredded coconut, optional

What to Do

1. Prepare a base for the pyramid. Two good choices: a large wooden cutting board, washed and dried, or a flat baking sheet wrapped in foil.
   - ⊙ Lay down eight graham-cracker squares to form an interconnecting square, with one square in the center.
   - ⊙ Break the remaining graham crackers and the chocolate bars into individual rectangles. With the vanilla mortar, thickly frost the bottom of several of the individual graham-cracker rectangles and begin building up the sides of the pyramid, moving in about ¼" from the sides of the bottom square.

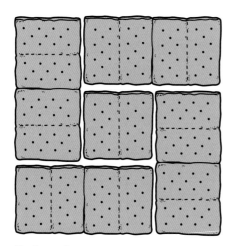

The base of the pyramid

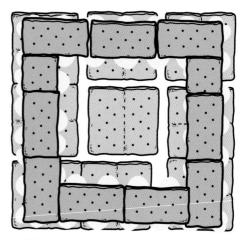

Building up the pyramid

2. On the second level, do the same, but begin interweaving a few chocolate pieces among the graham-cracker pieces. Continue working your way upward, stepping in about ¼" on each level, breaking the individual rectangles of graham cracker and chocolate into smaller bricks as needed to fit.

3. When you have built the walls up a few inches, use a spoon or rubber spatula to scrape the Marshmallow Fluff into the well in the center of the pyramid, then continue building the pyramid upward to enclose it. Gradually close off the top of the pyramid, using increasingly smaller graham crackers and chocolate bricks as needed to form the peak. Add plenty of mortar to help boost each level, so your pyramid isn't too flat.

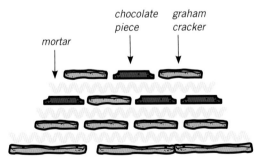

mortar   chocolate   graham
          piece   cracker

Construction Citations

For this particular project, it's preferable to be a little haphazard and slightly irregular as you go upward, spacing the bricks out by feel rather than geometry — and using lots of mortar. In effect, you want to "sculpt" your pyramid, molding it upward and smoothing out the sides with frosting as much as building it with graham-cracker "bricks." If you make it super-exact, you'll end up with a sharply stepped ziggurat, not a graceful upward-sloping pyramid.

4. When you're done with construction, it's time for facing the exterior. Thin out the mortar and use it liberally to coat the exterior of the pyramid, smoothing over any rough edges and filling in any gaps. Pull a knife up the sides to make a smooth surface.

5. For a sandy coating on the pyramid, pulse the vanilla wafers in a food processor or put them in a ziplock bag and roll over them with a rolling pin until they form fine crumbs. Leave a few coarser bits visible for texture. Spoon a handful into your palm and lightly press the crumbs against the frosted surface of the pyramid. Continue until no mortar is visible.

Fun Variation: Cover the outside of the pyramid with a thin layer of coconut. Cup your hand and scoop up some coconut, then press it lightly onto the sides, starting at the bottom and working your way up. The trick is to have too much in your hand so that the excess falls away. You can gather and reuse any excess as you work. When you're done, brush away any remaining excess. Surround the pyramid with light brown sugar.

6. Use a pastry brush to clear the crumbs from around the pyramid. To make the desert sand, put the granulated sugar in a plastic container with a lid, then add several drops of orange food coloring (or, to make orange: add six or eight drops of yellow food coloring and one or two drops of red). Cover tightly and shake until the orangey color is completely distributed throughout the sugar, and the color is even and smooth. Spoon the sugar sand in waves and mounds around the base of the pyramid.

The PALM TREES

What You'll Need

* Green Twizzlers from a pack of Rainbow Twizzlers
* Pretzel rods
* Vanilla Mortar (use leftovers from the Pyramid)

What to Do

1. For each tree trunk, break off a 2½" to 3" piece of pretzel rod. Use your finger to make a hole in the sugar "sand," and to deposit a little dollop of mortar into the hole. Push a pretzel-rod tree trunk into the hole (and mortar), and stand it upright. You may need to do a little jiggling or add a bit more mortar to get each tree trunk to balance securely.

2. To make the palm fronds:
   - For each tree cut a 2½" to 3" length of green Twizzler with scissors or a knife. Use a sharp knife to slice each piece in half lengthwise.
   - Use sharp kitchen shears to snip very gently along the edges of each half, to make a fringe. (You can skip this step, but it's a lot of bang for the effort!)
   - Put a tiny bit of mortar on top of each pretzel rod and lay one Twizzler frond on top, add more mortar, then lay on another Twizzler frond to crisscross the first. Balance the two fronds delicately, and let them sway there gently like a mobile. If you like, add a third palm-frond layer.

Blueprints

If you want to make all three of the large pyramids at Giza, two can have the same base size as the Great Pyramid, and should be stood close by one another, with one built shorter. For the best effect, make the third noticeably smaller (about half the size of the Great Pyramid) and set it farther away from the other two. Camels, to ferry the tourists, are optional.

PIRATE SHIP

With the canvas furled and an overflowing treasure chest already on board, these pirates are just sunning themselves in a hidden cove, not sailing the high seas looking for loot. But beware! Don't let the sweet stuff fool you. Their Jolly Roger flies high, and that cannon on deck is loaded for action.

Thanks to its lightweight frame and watertight base of Rice Krispies Treats, this ship is ready to grace the top of a cake — or serve as one, atop a platter bedecked with a blue-sugar sea. You can also pipe a thick frosting of blue ocean in lapping waves all around the base of the ship, and add a few leaping gummy fish for color.

If you want a more polished ship, frost the outside with Chocolate Mortar and press more candy into the sides. Pretzel squares make great stern windows.

The SHIP

MAKES 1 SHIP

What You'll Need

* Rice Krispies Treats, chocolate variation (see page 17), but following pouring instructions below
* Vanilla Mortar (see page 14) or 1 can store-bought white frosting
* Pretzel rods
* Fruit leather (preferably red or green)
* Licorice or caramel strings
* Black soft-eating licorice
* 1 square chocolate-covered candy (such as a caramel bonbon or mini candy bar)
* 1 Oreo Fun Stix or other cigar-shaped cookie
* Malted milk balls
* 1 (1.55-ounce) chocolate bar, such as Hershey's (the kind that is evenly divided into rectangles)
* Dots or M&Ms
* 1 Mini Oreo or other small round filled cookie
* Chocolate sprinkles
* Candy corn or jelly beans, optional

What to Do

1. Generously butter a 9" × 5" loaf pan. Prepare the Rice Krispies Treats as directed on page 17, and then pour the mixture into the prepared pan. Press and smooth down the mixture and let it cool.

2. To form the pirate ship:
   ⊙ When the rice mixture is cool, run a knife around the inside edges of the loaf pan and turn the whole loaf out onto a cutting board. Use a sharp chef's knife or a serrated knife to carefully slice down the sides, shaping the front quarter of the loaf into a triangular shape.

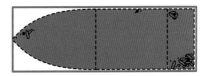

Trim the ship's hull off one end of the Rice Krispies Treats.

   ⊙ Carve out the central section of the ship: With the chef's knife or serrated knife, cut downward about 1" at either end of the center section, then carefully connect those two cuts by slicing a 1"-thick piece off the top of the loaf. Remove this piece to create the ship's lower deck.

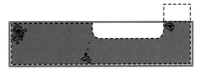

Cut out the lower deck and use the pieces to build up the stern.

Cut the removed piece in half and use them to build up the deck. Use mortar to attach a square at the back (the stern). Trim the other piece into a triangle and use mortar to fit it to the front (the bow).

3. Select a platter or cutting board to serve as the ship's base. You can use this as simply a place to build your ship (and later move it to a more permanent location), or you can serve the pirate ship directly from this base — your choice. Set the ship down on the base before moving on to the next step.

4. To make the mast pieces:
   - Use the same knife to carefully and gently hack out a slight V-shaped notch in the front of one pretzel rod, about halfway down the length. Be careful not to break the pretzel in half. Make a second notch about halfway between this notch and the top.
   - For the main crossbeam, take another pretzel rod and carefully carve out a notch about halfway down. Check that this beam will fit neatly up against the mast to form a cross.
   - For the top crossbeam, take a third pretzel rod and cut a piece off each end to make it about half the length of the

others. Trim another notch in it halfway across.

5. To attach and assemble the mast:
   - Gently push the bottom of the mast down into the center of the ship. (If your ship is very firm, you may need to open up a hole with the end of a wooden spoon.) Remove the mast, put mortar on its base, and push it gently into the hole until it stands up firmly.
   - Use a tiny dollop of mortar in each crossbeam notch and press the beams in place. Don't use too much, or the joints will be slippery instead of firm.

6. To make the sails, trim two lengths of fruit leather a little shorter than each crossbeam. Drape the sails lightly from each crossbeam, allowing them to hang down a bit, like sails that have been tied up. They may stick by themselves, but you can use a light coating of mortar on top of the beams. Use licorice or caramel string to tie the sails to the beam.

7. To make the Jolly Roger flag:
   - Roll and flatten a piece of black soft-eating licorice. Use a knife to trim it into a banner shape: wide at one side, slightly pointed, or notched to make two points, on the other.

Use a toothpick dipped in white mortar to trace the outlines of a tiny skull and crossbones onto the flag. You don't have to be too exact: the basic outlines will be easy to recognize when the flag is flying above the ship. Use your fingers to press one end of the flag around the top of the mast. The licorice should stick without mortar.

8. To make the cannon:
   ⊙ For the base, use a knife to hollow out a cradle in the square candy or mini candy bar. Angle the cut slightly upward, so the cannon will point outward and upward. (Ship's cannons are usually in solid bases like this, not on wheels, to prevent them from rolling across the deck.)
   ⊙ For the cannon, cut a 1½" length of the Fun Stix and lay it in the base.

(Use mortar to secure in place if necessary.) Set the cannon on the ship's lower deck, ready to be aimed and fired! Set some malted-milk cannon balls nearby.

9. To make a treasure chest:
   ⊙ Break off six rectangles from the chocolate bar. Lay two down to serve as the base of the treasure chest. Use mortar to stick two pieces upright along the long sides of the base piece.

- Use mortar to attach the remaining two chocolate pieces on each end. Position them on top of the base to hold the sides together.
- Fill the treasure chest with small bright candies, such as Dots or M&Ms. If you like, use another rectangle of chocolate as the lid; attach it with mortar, partially open, along one edge of the chest. Set the treasure chest on the bow of the ship.

10. To make the ship's wheel, apply mortar to the Mini Oreo around three-quarters of the edge. Push sprinkles upright into the mortar, so they stick out like spokes. Use a dab of mortar to glue the wheel upright to the prow.

The PIRATES

What You'll Need
* Licorice Allsorts (the layered kind, usually in cube shapes)
* Licorice strings
* Black and red soft-eating licorice
* Pretzel sticks
* Candy corn or jelly beans
* Vanilla Mortar (use leftovers from the Ship)
* Candy raspberries (such as Haribo), both red and black
* Green and red fruit leather

What to Do
1. To make each pirate's torso, use a chef's knife to trim the corners off a licorice Allsorts, and smooth the sides for a rounder shape.

2. For each pirate's arms:
   - Use a metal or bamboo skewer to carefully work a hole through the center of the torso, being careful not to break apart the Allsort layers. Make the hole just large enough to thread a length of licorice string through.
   - Cut a piece of licorice string about 3" long. Thread it through the hole in the torso.

3. For each pirate's legs, cut two pieces of red or black soft-eating licorice about 1½" long. Roll and shape the legs into rounds (this licorice is very pliable). If you like, break a pretzel stick in half and stick the broken end of each half into the bottom of the legs to form calves or a peg leg. Stick candy corn or jelly beans on the ends for the feet.

4. For each pirate's head:
- To make a headscarf, cut a narrow strip of fruit leather about 3" × ¼", and wrap it around the top of a Haribo raspberry. The leather is sticky enough that you don't need to use any mortar; just use the heat of your hand to mold it around the head. Twist the ends gently for the effect of a tied headscarf.
- For the eyes, pry out two red seeds from the face of the red berry, and replace it with two black seeds from the black berry.

5. To assemble each pirate, attach the top of the legs to the base of the torso with a bit of mortar. Use more mortar to stick the head on top of the torso. Trim the string arms a bit shorter if the body looks disproportionate.

MARTIAN-MALLOWS AND ALIENS

My two young sons came up with the idea of making Martian-Mallows, a concept that has since been kid-tested and approved by lots of little boys. Martian-Mallows are a great construction project for a group of small children, because anything goes. We'll start you off with a few standard alien creatures, to give kids the general idea, but don't be surprised when they quickly surpass the plan and come up with their own outrageous characters. The core of each alien is a frosted marshmallow, with or without coloring (or chocolate) in the icing, and from then on, it's open season: the more tentacles and waving arms, knobs, buttons, and protuberances, the better. Marshmallow aliens are fun to make in a group setting, and even more fun to eat.

INGREDIENTS BELOW WILL MAKE ALL THE CREATURES

What You'll Need

* Large marshmallows
* Vanilla Mortar (see page 14) or 1 can store-bought white frosting
* Chocolate or rainbow sprinkles
* Vanilla wafers or chocolate disks
* Red and black soft-eating licorice
* Candy raspberries (such as Haribo)
* Candy corn
* Dots or any small, round candy in multiple colors
* Chocolate chips
* Multicolored mini marshmallows
* Pull-N-Peel Twizzlers, optional

The TENTACULAR THREE-LEGGER

What to Do

1. To make the body, frost a large marshmallow on all sides with mortar, and roll it in sprinkles on all sides except the bottom. Set it on top of a vanilla wafer or chocolate disk.

2. To make the legs, smear a dollop of mortar on the bottom of the wafer or disk, and balance it on top of three upright pieces of soft-eating licorice. (You can give your alien two licorice legs, if you balance it with care, but three legs will allow it to stand up more securely.)

3. Poke a candy raspberry in the middle of the alien's face. (There should be enough mortar beneath the sprinkles that you won't have to add more to make it stick.)

4. To make tentacles, take a pair of scissors and cut a cylinder of soft-eating licorice in half. Snip lengthwise most of the way through one of the pieces, not quite to the bottom, making several cuts so that the licorice shreds into tentacles. Or simply use a length of Pull-N-Peel Twizzler and untwist the strands. Press the base of the tentacles on top of the marshmallow, pulling the tentacles apart for maximum effect.

The RADIATING-SPOKE CREATURE

What to Do

1. Frost a large marshmallow on all sides, and set it on top of a vanilla wafer or chocolate disk.

2. Stick six pieces of candy corn, points facing out, into the mortar. Arrange them in a straight line, radiating up the side and over the top.

3. To make eyes, stick on a pair of candy dots or chocolate chips. If you like, add a curved bit of red licorice for a mouth.

The AMORPHOUS BLOB

What to Do

1. Frost a marshmallow, then poke multi-colored mini marshmallows all over it.

2. Cover any remaining visible mortar with sprinkles.

3. Stick a candy raspberry or licorice head on top. If you want eyes, stick on two matching sprinkles with mortar.

The CHOCOLATE MENACE

What to Do

1. Frost a large marshmallow on all sides, and set it on top of a chocolate disk.

2. Press another chocolate disk on top, curved side up.

3. Press chocolate chips in a ring around the marshmallow.

4. Glue two red eyes snipped from the end of a piece of red licorice just below the rim of the top disk. Two red Dots will also work well as eyes. If you like, trim a slice off either side of another chocolate disk and stick them into the sides of the marshmallows as arms.

FAIRY-TALE CASTLE

There's some leeway with castle design: You can make just a crenellated castle façade with two side walls as props. Or, if you want to take your degree in candy architectural engineering, you can square the façade and make a freestanding unit with a castle keep inside. However you choose to build, your statuesque towers — made of cookies and topped with decorated cones — will be fit for a king (or princess or knight errant)!

You can experiment with many kinds of square or rectangular cookies, but filled wafer cookies (the ones with a waffle surface and a stiff cream filling inside) have very square edges and fit together just like bricks. Wafer sizes differ, so you may need a few cookies more or less as you build. What's more, they come in vanilla, chocolate, and strawberry flavors, so you can make your castle tan, brown, or pink, as you prefer. Build your masterpiece on a large wooden cutting board, or wrap a sheet of plywood in tinfoil, shiny side out, so you can easily move your castle to its rightful (prominent!) place.

The CASTLE

What You'll Need

* 2 packages filled wafer cookies
* Chocolate or Vanilla Mortar (see page 14) or 1 can store-bought frosting
* 1 (8" x 4") pound cake (the kind found in the frozen-dessert section of the supermarket)
* 2 graham crackers
* 1 (1.55-ounce) chocolate bar, such as Hershey's (the kind that are evenly divided into rectangles)
* Chocolate-covered pretzel rounds or star-shaped cookies
* Candy for decorating: jelly beans, candy sticks, licorice string, sour strips, gum tape, mini cookies (any color or shape that's not too heavy to hang on a wafer wall with frosting mortar)
* 2 (18-ounce) packages round sandwich cookies (such as Oreos or Golden Oreos)
* Ice cream cones (the pointy kind)
* Pink and red colored sugar
* Fruit leather
* Additional white or brown chocolate bars or nonpareils, optional
* Gumdrops, lollipops, and gummy fish or crocodiles, optional

What to Do

1. To build the walls of the keep (the interior building, with four walls and three towers):
   ⊙ Select a platter or cutting board to serve as your work surface and, ultimately, your castle's base.

⊙ With the wafer cookies lying flat on the work surface, use mortar to build two side walls that are two wafer cookies wide and nine cookies high. Mortar the thin sides of the cookies, as shown.

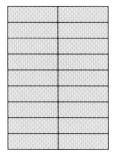

Side walls of the keep, two cookies wide

⊙ Build the keep front and back as if you were laying bricks: alternate rows of two whole cookies with rows of one whole cookie flanked by two halves. (When cutting the cookies in half, use a sharp chef's knife). Again, mortar the thin sides of the cookies.

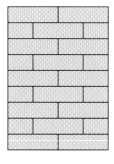

Front wall of the keep, alternating whole and half cookies

2. To make the blocks (or piers) that prop up the interior corners of the keep: mortar three wafer cookies together on their wide flat tops. Repeat with a second set of three cookies, and then mortar these two stacks together vertically, to form a wafer cookie pier. Repeat to make three more piers, one for each corner of the keep.

Interior supporting pier

3. To raise the walls of the keep:

⊚ Pick up the front wall and mortar it against the wafer sides of the two piers, flush with the outer edges. There should be a pier at either corner, with the filling edges of the wafer cookies exposed on the sides of the keep.

⊚ When the wall is upright, mortar on the two side walls, pressing them against the filling edges of the support piers and securing them with mortar as needed.

⊚ Take the two remaining support piers and secure their filling edges to the back corners of the keep's side walls with mortar.

⊚ Pick up the back wall and mortar it against the wafer sides of the two back piers. You now have a stable four-walled interior keep for your castle.

⊚ To add the central tower, you will need a roof on your keep. Trim the pound cake to the same height as your keep and cut the ends flat so that it will stand upright. Use mortar to stand the cake in the center of the keep, then mortar two whole graham crackers side by side to the top of the cake. They will hang over the sides of the cake. This roof will support the central tower.

4. To build the exterior walls:

⊚ Build the exterior front wall as if you were laying bricks: alternate rows of three whole cookies with rows of two whole cookies flanked by two halves. (When cutting the cookies in half, use a sharp chef's knife.) Again, mortar the thin sides of the cookies.

⊚ Use six rectangles of the candy bar as a guide to cut out the front door of the castle: place the candy bar sections over the lower middle section of the front wall and cut around it with a sharp chef's knife. Set aside the chocolate door for later.

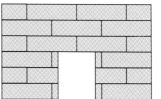

Exterior front wall with door cut out

- Make two side walls that are the same dimensions as the front wall. Do not cut doors from the side walls.

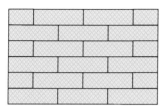

Exterior side walls, built using the brick-laying method

5. To crenellate the façades, cut wafer cookies into individual blocks and decorate them with jelly beans or other small candies. Use mortar to attach the decorations, and then more mortar to stand the pieces on the top of the façades.

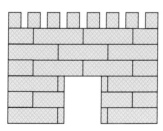

Crenellated facade

Fun Variation: Almost any flat candy can be used to crenellate your castle. Try white or milk Hershey rectangles cut in half or, for a scalloped look, nonpareils cut in half.

6. To decorate the façades, use mortar to add rows of any bright candy you like, from jelly beans marching along the castle's base to licorice string or a glittering strip of sugary sour tape outlining the central doorway. Chocolate-covered pretzel rounds make good windows. Be careful not to make your décor too heavy: this wall will have to stand up soon. A few rows of color and sugary glitter are a better bet than encrusting the entire surface with candy.

7. To build the towers:
- For the two exterior towers, mortar together 12 sandwich cookies in a tall stack for each tower. Don't use too much mortar: a little bit will glue them securely, while too much may make the cookies slip.
- For the two front keep towers, mortar together two stacks of 15 sandwich cookies. If you like, put shorter stacks of three to four cookies on the corners of the graham-cracker keep roof.
- Build a central tower with three sandwich cookies and mortar. Or vary the towers by using a different type of cookie for the central tower.

8. To put the castle all together, you may need a second pair of hands:

- Raise the front wall (it should stand upright without breaking, though a few candies may fall off) 2" to 3" in front of the castle keep.
- Slather mortar along the outside edge of one end of each side wall and in a straight line down the outer wafer side at the front end of each wall. Attach the side castle walls to the façade, then carefully press the outer towers against the strip of mortar on the side walls.
- Put the two inner towers alongside the corners of the castle keep, firmly anchoring them with a dab of mortar to the keep walls.

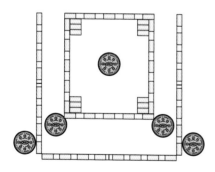

9. To make the turrets, spread a thin layer of frosting on five ice cream cones and roll them in colored sugar. Cut flags from fruit leather and fly them from the pointy ends of the cones. Turn the cones upside down on top of the towers; a dollop of icing on the edges of the top cookie will hold everything together.

10. Add the drawbridge:

- Lay your chocolate door shape in front of the castle door; this is your drawbridge.
- Cut two lengths of licorice string to serve as the raising chains. Glue them to either side of the door frame with mortar. Add hard candies to hide the attachment point.
- Drape the lower ends of the strings down to the outer edges of the draw-bridge; secure them with a bit of mortar and then glue each down underneath a piece of candy.

11. Embellish! Now that the castle is con-structed, let your imagination take over. Some options:

- Wrap a bright stripe of sour strip around the base of each turret.
- Put candy sticks along the corners to hide the seams. Top with gumdrop flowers.
- People the castle with princesses made from gumdrops and fruit leather.
- Put a fruit leather moat around the cas-tle and add gummy fish or crocodiles.
- Plant lollipop trees on the grounds.

Construction Citations

The only way to make your castle better is to make it . . . bigger. If you've got the cookies, candy, and time, you can square the walls and make a fully three-dimensional castle. Double the keep and quadruple the castle plans. (Build the keep first, obviously, so you can enclose it with the finished castle outer wall.) Put a tower at each of the eight corners, and build more of the interior piers to add support at each corner. Your impressive structure will be even more imposing.

On the other hand, if you're short on time, build the front façade only by following the instructions in steps 4, 5, and 6. Then build the two front towers in step 7 and put it all together.

4

We all know that candy is fun, and we all know that games and toys are fun. So what happens when we use candy to *make* toys and games? The projects that follow are triply terrific: fun to make, fun to play with, and (of course) fun to eat. Did childhood just get better, or what?

BOARD GAMES

You can purchase molds to form your own edible checkerboard and playing pieces out of chocolate. But you can also bake one up very quickly from luscious cakey blondies and brownies. A little trimming, a little arranging (ideal work for small fingers) and you've got a playing board that's ready for action.

To make checkers, you merely need two different colors of miniature cookies. You can make other board games — anything that's played on a checkerboard — with basic candy pieces. You can really let your imagination loose when it comes to creating chess pieces.

For an even surface on your game board, make these brownies and blondies without any additions such as nuts or chocolate or butterscotch chips. On their own, both recipes result in cakelike, moist baked goods that lend themselves to lying flat as you construct your checkerboard. But they'll be equally delicious and just as functional (if a bit bumpier) with any add-ins that you like, so if you love walnuts in your brownies and pecans in your blondies, don't be shy!

One-Pot Blondies

MAKES 36 (1¹/₃″) SQUARES

What You'll Need:

½ cup (1 stick) butter

1 cup light brown sugar

2 eggs

1½ teaspoons vanilla

½ teaspoon baking powder

¼ teaspoon baking soda

¼ teaspoon salt

1 cup flour

What to Do:

1. Preheat oven to 350°F. Lightly grease a 9" × 9" baking pan. Cut a square of parchment paper to fit, and line the bottom of the pan.

2. Melt the stick of butter in a large saucepan over medium-low heat, being careful not to let it sizzle or burn. Remove the pan from the heat before the entire stick has melted and whisk in the brown sugar; the remaining butter will melt as you stir.

3. Whisk in the eggs and vanilla. Stir in the baking powder, baking soda, and salt with a wooden spoon. When fully combined, add the flour and mix just to combine. Pour immediately into the prepared pan and bake for 17 minutes, until just set and lightly golden.

Blueprints

If you like, add 1 cup chopped pecans or butterscotch chips (or 1/2 cup of each) after stirring in the flour in Step 3. Using light brown sugar instead of dark helps keep the contrast as strong as possible between the light and dark squares on the finished game board.

4. Cool blondies in the pan for 10 minutes, then turn out onto a wire rack and cool completely.

GAME BOARD

MAKES 1 CHECKERBOARD,

APPROXIMATELY 12″ × 12″

What You'll Need
* 1 pan of One-Pot Blondies (see page 89)
* 1 pan of One-Pot Brownies (see page 18)

Note: Hersheys makes a "Special Dark" cocoa that's now widely available. It's half dark cocoa powder and half Dutch-process cocoa, which is alkalized to remove some of the acid and bitterness. It has a noticeably darker color and smoother, richer flavor than regular cocoa. Conveniently enough, it also makes your brownies a deep, dark, glossy brown that's a perfect contrast to the golden blondies.

Construction Citations

If you have two 9″ × 9″ baking pans, you can make these two recipes almost simultaneously. First mix the blondies in the saucepan, and pour them into a prepared pan. Then mix the brownies in the same saucepan without washing it. (Make the blondies first so they won't have chocolate streaks from the brownie batter.)

If you don't have two 9″ × 9″ pans, make the blondies first anyway. After the first 10 minutes of baking time, start mixing up the brownies in the blondies saucepan. When the blondies come out of the oven, cool them for a few minutes. Then, using oven mitts, hold a cooling rack directly over the pan and turn both over. The blondies will slip easily out of the pan and onto the cooling rack. Cover them with a second cooling rack and invert so they're right side up, and remove the top rack. You don't want them to cool with crosshatchings on top from the rack.

Now, lay a fresh square of parchment paper in the bottom of the hot pan, pour in the brownie batter, and bake. You'll be ready to say "King me!" before you know it.

What to Do

1. Bake the blondies and brownies that will make up your alternating squares, then construct the board while they're still slightly warm. This makes them more pliable and allows you to shape them into a tighter and flatter game board. Transfer the uncut brownies and blondies from the cooling rack to a large cutting board.

2. To cut the squares:
- Using a serrated bread knife or a sharp chef's knife, trim off and discard (i.e., eat) about ¼" from each of the four edges of the blondies and brownies.
- Cut the trimmed square into 36 equal squares, each about 1⅓" wide. There's no need to measure: you can eyeball it and still get good results. Just cut exactly down the center of the original square, then divide each half into three equal parts. Turn the cutting board 90 degrees and do it again.

3. Prepare a base for your game board. If you slide each batch of freshly cut brownies and blondies off your cutting board onto waiting sheets of waxed paper, you can use the cutting board as the base, with or without a foil or waxed-paper liner. A flat or rimmed baking sheet, lined or not, is also a good choice.

4. Build the checkerboard by alternating light and dark squares: eight down, eight across. You'll need 32 squares of each color, leaving four leftovers of each color — so you can pick and choose a little if one square is too flat or taller than the others. Ideally, you'll put thinner pieces at the outer edges of your checkerboard, with slightly puffier pieces in the center.

5. Nudge the pieces firmly together with your hands as you build the checkerboard, but don't squash them. When you're done, if your board isn't level enough for your taste, you can even it out by laying a sheet of waxed paper or plastic wrap over the whole checkerboard (if you're worried about sticking, spray it lightly with cooking spray first), then lay a baking sheet or second cutting board on top. Press down firmly with your hands, exerting equal pressure across the surface as best you can. Instantly and carefully peel off the waxed paper or plastic wrap and let your board air-cool at room temperature, uncovered, while you prepare your game pieces. (Don't worry: The squares will still taste good!)

FOR CHESS

What You'll Need

* 16 Hershey's Kisses (dark color)
* 16 Hershey's Hugs (white color)
* 16 candy "bases" of varying heights and kinds (such as licorice Allsorts, caramels, or coconut squares)
* Chocolate or Vanilla Mortar (see page 14) or 1 can store-bought frosting
* Chocolate-covered bonbons, marshmallows, or mini peanut butter cups, optional

What to Do

1. Pawns are simple: a row of Hershey's Kisses, dark on one side and white on the other.

2. To make the second row of pieces, you can use your imagination. Start each piece with a base made up of differing candies, then stick a dark or white Kiss on the top with mortar, to avoid confusion between sides.

   * Rooks could be square licorice Allsorts, crowned with a Kiss of the proper color, or bishops could be a Kiss atop a chocolate-covered bonbon.
   * Knights could start with a marshmallow on the bottom.
   * Kings and Queens could incorporate mini peanut-butter-cup crowns.
   * Rummage through your own candy shop and see what fun (and yummy) combos you can come up with.

3. Once you've made your various pieces (just make sure each incorporates the right Hug or Kiss), you're ready to play. If you don't know the rules, check your Hoyle's or type "how to play chess" into your favorite Internet search engine.

FOR CHECKERS

What You'll Need

* 12 mini chocolate sandwich cookies, such as Mini Oreos
* 12 mini light-colored sandwich cookies, such as Mini Golden Oreos or Nutter Butters Bites

Construction Citations

Each player lines up the cookies on the light squares only (the blondies). When a checker is jumped and removed from the board, it becomes fair game, but don't eat all your lawful prey at once — you may need to reserve a few, lest your opponent makes it to the back row. Then you'll need a cookie crown to signify that piece has been "kinged."

Note: You can use any small, flat contrasting cookies for checkers: 12 oatmeals versus 12 chocolate chips, for example.

FOR OTHELLO

What You'll Need

* 32 each of two contrasting mini sandwich cookies (such as Mini Oreos, and Mini Golden Oreos or Nutter Butter Bites)

What to Do

1. To make opposable cookie pieces, take one light and one dark miniature sandwich cookie. Pry off one side of each, and stick it onto the other cookie. Repeat until all 32 cookies are light on one side and dark on the other.

2. Each player chooses a color, and you're ready to play. Check your Hoyle's or type "how to play Othello" into your favorite Internet search engine.

> **Note:** You may know this game under the brand name Othello, but its generic name is Reversi. The super-simple rules belie the game's complexity, which requires you to assess your opponent's strategy and plan ahead as you battle for control of the board.

ARM CANDY

The jewel tones of fruit Life Savers are ideal for bracelets and neck-laces, but any candy with a hole in it can be strung on a licorice-string and personalized with any child's favorite color scheme. (Wint-O-Green Life Savers, with the shiny mint flecks, have a pearly iridescence that makes them ideal for evening wear.) For individual flair, make a pendant necklace by hanging any shape of gummy candy in the center of a necklace-length licorice string. Or make a charm bracelet by stringing Life Savers alternated with a favorite shape of cereal or gummies. One last thing: Don't expect this project to please only girls. Very few little boys are averse to a string of readily edible candy around their wrists or necks!

Children won't be bored for a long time with stringing candy, but grownups might want to mix things up a bit. Then it's time to turn on the oven and make candy pendants. There are two ways to go about forming a candy pendant or charm: the pretzel method, which results in a natural hole for hanging; or the freeform melted pendant, where you need to make the hole with a skewer in the hot jewelry. Either way, your candy necklace will glow with style!

▼▼▼▼▼▼▼▼▼▼▼
BRACELET

MAKES 1 BRACELET

What You'll Need
* 12 inches licorice string in black or red (such as Twizzler's Pull-n-Peel) or caramel string
* Life Savers or any round candy with a hole
* Mini Life Savers or round colored cereal (such as Froot Loops)
* Gummy candy, any shape, or chocolate coins

What to Do
1. Thread Life Savers on the licorice string, creating patterns with color and by alternating them with mini Life Savers or Froot Loops. Try all one color of each, or one Life Saver followed by three Froot Loops — anything you like.

Construction Citations
Kids can thread the candy on the bracelets, but if they want to hang a few "charms," a grownup can help to poke holes in the gummy candy.

2. If you like, add charms made from gummy candy or chocolate coins. You can use a metal or wooden skewer to carefully bore a hole, and then wiggle the skewer to enlarge it. Gently push the licorice through the hole. It might stick a little, but don't be tempted to make the hole too big or the charm may break too easily and drop off the string.

3. With the bracelet in place on the child's wrist, have a grownup tie a loose granny knot in the licorice ends. Leave it loose enough for the bracelet to slide on and off the wrist easily while holding the candy in place. (The wearer retains the option to bite the candy off as needed — but, with a loose knot, there's also the more tooth-friendly choice of untying the bracelet to slide off a piece.)

Blueprints

A strand from a Twizzler's Pull-n-Peel is just about the right length to make a bracelet for a child's wrist, including the knot, but necklaces are a little bit more difficult. They need to lift easily on and off over the child's head, so the necklace string should be about 24″ in length.

Caramel string from Ikea is perfect for the candy-jewelry studio. It's hollow and quite firm, so it's a bit sturdier than licorice string. This allows you to make necklaces that won't break from the weight of the candy you string on it. If you don't have an Ikea nearby, you can nonetheless make longer necklaces by knotting two pieces of licorice rope with a granny knot. String the candy from either end, then finish with a second knot.

WRISTWATCH

What You'll Need

* 1 egg white*
* 2 tablespoons confectioners' sugar
* 2 gummy orange slices
* 8 inches tape gum or sour candy strips
* Fruit-flavored licorice twists (or gum strips in a complementary color)
* Melted chocolate or decorating gel, optional

> * There is a slight risk of Salmonella or other foodborne illness when using raw eggs. If you are concerned, you can use pasteurized egg white or 2 teaspoons of powdered egg white mixed with 2 tablespoons water in place of the raw egg white.

Construction Citations

These instructions make a wristwatch that's fun to eat and look at, but can be difficult to wear. If your child wants to wear the watch, cut the gum strip long enough to tie the ends loosely around the child's wrist (about 12" to 14").

What to Do

1. Whisk the egg white with the confectioners' sugar until just foamy. This is your watchmaker's glue; it dries almost clear.

2. Use scissors or a small knife to cut the bottom off of each gummy orange slice, making the ends flat. The aim is to stick them together to make an even circle to form the watch face. Paint each cut side with a little egg-white glue and press the cut sides together. (You may want to hold them together with a toothpick inserted across the two halves until they dry.)

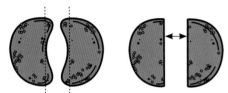

Trim two orange slices to have straight edges.

Glue the cut sides together to form the watch face.

3. Use scissors to cut a rounded end on the gum or sour strip wristband, and then use a metal skewer, toothpick, or hole punch to poke four or five holes in that end.

4. Paint the center of the strip with a little glue and press on the gummy watch face. While it dries, use scissors to cut strips of fruit-flavored licorice into two little hands, plus 12 number markers for the face. Using a pair of tweezers, dip each piece into the glue before positioning it on the watch face. (It helps to have a damp paper towel to wipe the end of the tweezers after you position each piece, to keep the next piece from sticking to the tweezers.)

> **Easy Variation:** You can also paint the numbers and hands on the watch face with melted chocolate or decorating gel.

5. Cut longer strips of colored licorice to form the clasp. Dip them into the glue and stick in place (see photo).

STAINED GLASS PENDANTS

What You'll Need

* Pretzel twists
* Multicolored hard candy or Life Savers
* Caramel or licorice string
* Froot Loops, optional

What to Do

1. Preheat the oven to 325°F and line a baking sheet with parchment paper (not waxed paper) or a Silpat. You can also use foil; just turn it shiny side up and spray it lightly with baking spray.

2. Lay the pretzel twists flat on the lined baking sheet.

3. Unwrap three or four of each hard candy color you're using, and seal each color in a ziplock bag. Using the bottom of a

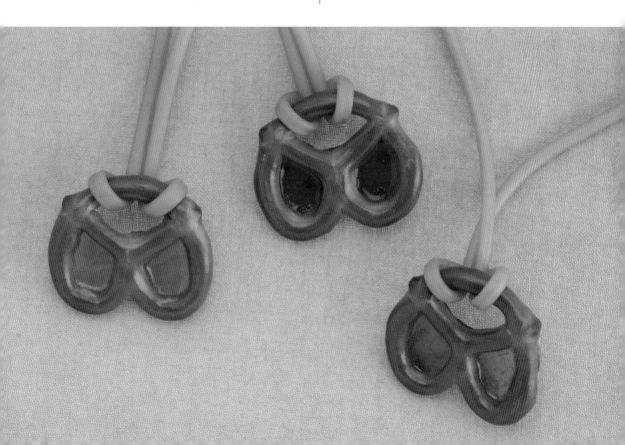

mug or sturdy drinking glass, pound the candies into powder.

4. Bake the pendants:

- Use a small spoon to mound a generous amount of one color into each of the two lower segments of the pretzel twist. Or simply place a spoonful of crushed candy on the baking sheet and nestle the pretzel on top, brushing away the excess. Whatever method you choose, be sure that a generous amount of candy is in contact with the lower segments of the pretzel and that the small, central opening is empty. Don't worry about using too much candy; you can break off excess pieces when it cools.

- Place the baking sheet in the oven and bake for 3 to 4 minutes, just until the hard-candy powder melts. Keep a close eye on the pretzels to make sure they don't burn. Remove the tray from the oven and carefully slide the parchment paper, silicone mat, or aluminum foil off the baking sheet so the candy doesn't continue to melt.

Fun Variation: If you like, tie a knot in the licorice on either side of the pendant and then loop Froot Loops or Life Savers on either side. The knots keep the other candies from bumping up against your delicate stained-glass pendant.

5. String the pendants on a caramel or licorice string, with the string running through the small empty eye in the central pretzel twist.

JEWEL-TONE DROP PENDANTS

What You'll Need

* Multicolored hard candy or Life Savers
* Caramel or licorice string

Construction Citations

Start simply, with pools of color, until you get used to working with the melted candy, and then start working your way up to multicolored drops.

What to Do

1. Preheat the oven to 325°F and line a baking sheet with parchment paper (not waxed paper) or a Silpat. If you want to use foil, turn it shiny side up and spray it lightly with baking spray.

2. Lay different colored whole candies or Life Savers flat on the lined baking sheet or crush the candy into powder and sprinkle it thickly inside a metal cookie cutter placed on the baking sheet. The photograph on this page shows a pendant made in a heart-shaped cutter. Bake for 4 to 5 minutes, watching carefully, until each candy melts into a pool of color. Don't walk away or the candy may bubble and scorch.

3. Remove the baking sheet from the oven as soon as the candies melt and start to spread. While they are still warm and soft (within 1 to 2 minutes of removing them from the heat), use a metal or bamboo skewer, or a knife tip, to gently make a small hole in the melted candy, in the center or to one side. Allow to cool completely.

4. String the pendant on a caramel or licorice string. If you're stringing other

pendants or candies next to it, tie a knot on either side of the pendant to protect it.

Variations

When you've gotten the hang of the melting and the hole-poking, sass up your pendants with cool variations by putting dots of other colored candies up against your central pieces. These can be so pretty that you won't even want to eat them — but you can!

⊙ Crush a yellow Life Saver into chunks and lay those chunks on the baking sheet around an orange Life Saver. Make sure the yellow pieces are touching each other and the orange piece. When it all melts, you'll have a glowing orange center surrounded by a yellow halo.

⊙ To make an apple shape, put a chunk of green Life Saver up against a red whole Life Saver. This will melt into a green stem for a red apple.

⊙ Make a bunch of grapes by arranging six purple Life Savers as shown, with half a green Life Saver on top for a stem.

⊙ You can make a flower by putting chunks of one Life Saver color at intervals around another color, always touching the central piece. The chunks should not touch each other; they will melt into petals around the central color.

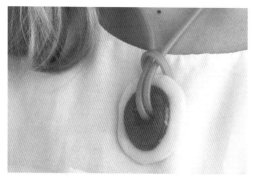

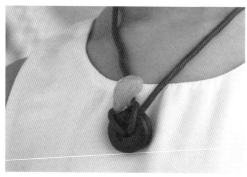

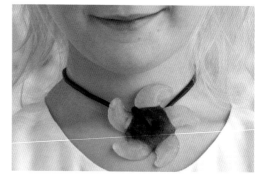

CANDY SUSHI

A little piece of cake, wrapped in fruit leather and topped with coconut, makes an astonishingly realistic plate of sushi. If you find dark green fruit leather among the increasingly lurid colors available, your sushi will look even more convincing.

Tiny bento boxes are increasingly easy to find at gourmet stores. When it's not filled with candy sushi, it makes a fun container to pack your child's lunch in!

BENTO BOX

What You'll Need

* Doughnut holes (you use one for each piece of sushi; make as many as you like!)
* Vanilla Mortar (see page 14) or 1 can store-bought white frosting
* Green and red fruit leather

* Flake coconut
* Gummy shapes in red or orange
* Green fruit chews (such as Starburst)
* 1–2 tablespoons cola (or molasses), optional
* Pink fruit leather, optional

What to Do

1. To make each sushi piece, take a thin slice off the top and bottom of the doughnut hole to level it, but don't cut it too thin. Put a thin layer of vanilla frosting over the top and around the sides of the doughnut hole.

2. Wrap a narrow slice of green fruit leather around the frosted sides, pressing the ends together to stick. Don't let the top edge of the leather curl down over the doughnut; keep it standing up straight like a piece of nori (the seaweed that wraps sushi).

3. To mimic sushi rice, sprinkle the frosted top of the doughnut hole thickly with coconut. You can press it lightly into the frosting but try to keep it within the bounds of the fruit leather without collapsing the edges.

4. Use a small gummy shape (little fish are ideal) or trim a larger shape as desired, and press it into the coconut topping.

5. Make as much candy sushi as you like, perhaps a double row of 6 or 8 on a Japanese-looking plate. To complete the presentation:

⊙ Slice little pieces of red (or better, pink) fruit leather and mound them together loosely on the plate, to look like pickled ginger.

⊙ Unwrap a green fruit chew and heat for 10 to 15 seconds (no more!) in the microwave. It will soften just enough for you to press and mold it into a little triangular mound that looks like wasabi paste. Put it next to the pickled ginger.

⊙ If you have a small soy sauce dish like the ones in Japanese restaurants, pour a tablespoon of cola (or molasses) into it and place it next to the plate.

⊙ Chopsticks are optional!

Blueprints

For a mound of wasabi paste that doesn't come out of the microwave, use a small segment of a green Twizzler. Use your hands to knead it into a small wasabi shape.

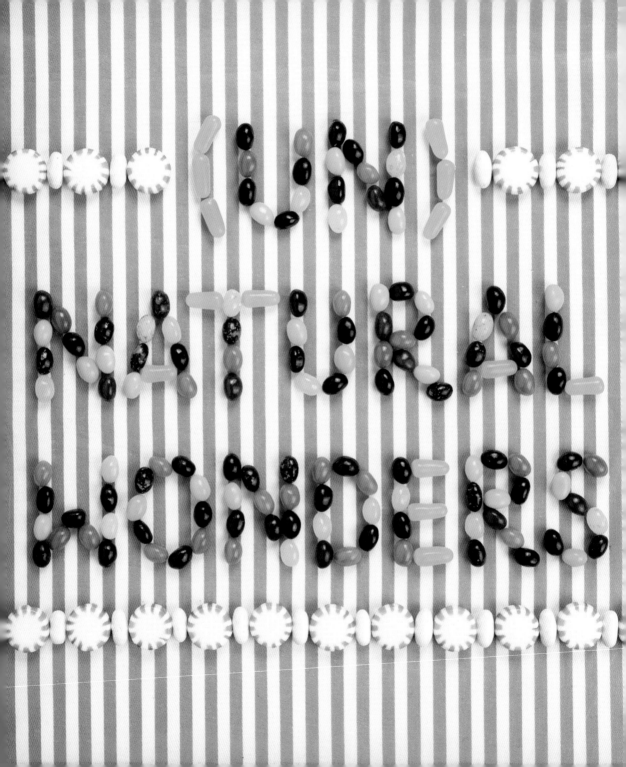

Okay, candy may not be the most natural of foods, but you can still get in touch with your nature-loving side through the magic of candy construction. Licorice laces, gummy worms, colored-candy dots, strips, and stripes all lend themselves to the re-creation of little critters, whether they be crawly or cute. Added bonus: Kids can amaze their friends by chomping down a sugary centipede or savoring a slithery snake!

CREEPY-CRAWLIES

Bugs with lots of legs and waving antennae can be kind of creepy, unless those legs are licorice! And the pretty colors on a butterfly's wings are even more beautiful when they gleam like stained glass, made from melted hard candies in jewel tones. Candy bugs are similar to candy jewelry in that they use lots of candy string and stained glass, but the results are deliciously creepy-crawly.

STAINED-GLASS BUTTERFLIES

What You'll Need

* Pretzel twists, regular or mini
* Life Savers or other hard candies in several colors (such as red, yellow, green, and orange)
* Vanilla Mortar (see page 14) or 1 can store-bought white frosting
* Chocolate disks (such as Droste) or vanilla wafers
* Sour gummy worms (the brightly colored, sugar-coated ones)
* Nerds, dragees, or other tiny round candy

What to Do

1. Preheat the oven to 325°F and line a baking sheet with parchment paper (not waxed paper) or a Silpat. You can also use foil, just turn it shiny side up and spray it lightly with baking spray.

Construction Citations

Waxed paper is not a suitable substitute for parchment: the wax melts and the candy ends up sticking to the paper underneath. If you don't have parchment paper or a silicone baking-sheet liner, you can also use foil. Turn it shiny side up and smooth it with your hand, pressing it against the baking sheet so nothing can stick in any crevice. It also helps to spray it lightly with baking spray or rub on a little bit of butter or oil, just enough to film the foil. This makes it easier to peel off, should the melted candy stick slightly.

2. Lay the pretzel twists flat on the lined baking sheet.

3. Unwrap three or four of each hard candy color you're using, and seal each color in a separate ziplock bag. Pound the candies into powder with the bottom of a heavy mug or glass.

4. Bake the butterflies:
   - Use a small spoon to mound a generous amount of one color into each of the two lower segments of the pretzel twist. Or simply place a spoonful of crushed candy on the baking sheet and nestle the pretzel down into the candy, brushing away the excess. Whatever method you choose, be sure that a generous amount of candy is in contact with the pretzel. Don't worry about using too much candy; you can break off excess pieces when it cools.
   - Place the baking sheet in the oven and bake for 3 to 4 minutes, just until the hard-candy powder melts. Keep a close eye on the pretzels to make sure they don't burn. Remove the tray from the oven and carefully slide the parchment paper, silicone mat, or aluminum foil off the baking sheet so the candy doesn't continue to melt.

5. Put a thick dollop of mortar in the center of a chocolate disk or vanilla wafer. Center a sour gummy worm in the mortar and press it in to secure it. Press a pretzel wing into the mortar on either side of the worm, anchoring them firmly. Tip them upright or lay them flat as you prefer. If you wish to add eyes, use a dab of frosting to stick on two Nerds at the head of the worm.

Blueprints

Use an individual butterfly to top a cupcake, or make a platter full of them, about to take flight. The chocolate disk or vanilla wafer beneath anchors the butterfly and lets the wings stand up nicely. If you're using your butterfly on a cupcake, you can skip the support disk and position the wings right on the frosting.

⌐CENTIPEDES and MILLIPEDES

What You'll Need

* Caramel string or licorice string (such as Twizzler's Pull-n-Peel)
* Life Savers or other round candy with a hole
* Royal Icing Glue (see page 16)
* Mini Dots or other small round candy

What to Do

1. Cut a length of caramel or licorice string and tie a knot gently in one end of the string, just big enough to keep the candy from falling off. Use another string (of a different color, if desired) to cut several strands about 3" long to serve as legs.

2. Start sliding Life Savers loosely onto the main string, varying the colors to make a pattern, or stringing them on in a motley array. After every three Life Savers, tie one of the leg strings around the central string, leaving the ends hanging downward. Then push the Life Savers up against it and continue until your critter is as long as you like.

3. When you reach the end, knot the string gently again, being careful not to pull so hard that you break it.

4. Select one end for the front, and use a dab of royal icing to glue on two Mini Dot eyes. Use a toothpick to dab royal icing pupils on the eyes. Tie additional string just behind the head to serve as antennae, but turn this knot so that the strands point upward.

5. Trim the legs so that they're even, to give a better impression of waving centipede legs.

CANDY SNAKES

What You'll Need

* Bubble-gum tape or sour strips
* Necco wafers
* Green hard candies (such as Life Savers)
* Royal Icing Glue (see page 16)
* Mini Dots
* Licorice string

What to Do

1. To make the body, cut a piece of gum tape about 6" long. On the front end, use scissors or a paring knife to trim the tip into the forked tongue of a snake.

2. Preheat the oven to 350°F and line a baking sheet with parchment paper (not waxed paper) or a silicone liner (such as Silpat). You can also use foil, just turn it shiny side up and spray it lightly with baking spray.

3. To make the snake's scales:
   ⊙ For each snake, place six Necco wafers on a baking sheet.
   ⊙ Unwrap the hard candies and put several in a ziplock bag. Crush them into crumbs with the bottom of a heavy mug or glass. Sprinkle a few shards of

crushed candy onto each Necco wafer and bake for 3 to 4 minutes, just until the hard candy melts into the wafers. Slide the parchment paper, silicone mat, or foil off the baking sheet and let cool.

⊙ Brush icing along the length of the tape and layer on the cooled Necco wafers in an overlapping pattern.

4. To make the snake's eyes, cut small slits in the centers of the Mini Dots and press short pieces of licorice string into the slits. Smooth a bit of icing on the first Necco wafer after the tongue and glue on the Mini Dots.

Construction Citations

If you're letting a group of kids make candy snakes as a craft activity, supply each child with a ziplock bag in which to carry the snake home afterward. Cut the tapes no longer than the ziplock, so the snake can slither in whole and lie flat. That way, even if some of the candies slip off, the whole thing will stay together in the bag until a child can get it home and reassemble any scales the snake has sloughed off.

WOODLAND CREATURES

It's quiet and peaceful out in the forest, nothing stirring, not a sound — until you start to look around. Then you'll see wildlife everywhere: little white baby bunnies fast asleep, owls blinking from the treetops, field mice skittering away. An alarmed porcupine hustles into the underbrush, and out hops a googly-eyed frog with spots that say "Don't touch!" Oh wait, they're all actually made of a sweet, truffle-like candy that's literally good enough to eat.

The white chocolate dough is yummy, but you can also make any of the creatures with the Peanut Butter Play Dough or Chocolate Play Dough on page 19. For the best look, roll the bunnies thickly and thoroughly in the sugar, but let the field mice be a bit more mottled, without complete sugar coverage.

White Chocolate Dough

MAKES ABOUT 2½ CUPS

What You'll Need:

24 vanilla wafers

6 ounces (1 cup) white chocolate chips

¼ cup sour cream

What to Do:

1. Crush the vanilla wafers to crumbs in a food processor. Or you can seal them in a ziplock bag and use a rolling pin to beat and roll them to crumbs.

2. Melt the white chocolate chips by placing them in a medium-size glass bowl and melting in the microwave on high for 1 minute. Whisk well with a fork. If any lumps remain, heat in 10-second blasts, stirring well after each. Be careful not to overheat, or the mixture will scorch or seize.

3. Stir the crumbs into the melted chips, mixing until well combined. Then stir in the sour cream, blending well.

4. Chill the mixture for 15 to 20 minutes, no more, just until it's stiff enough to handle, but not too cold. If you leave it in the fridge too long, soften it until workable by giving the mixture short blasts in the microwave, about 20 seconds at a time, stirring well after each.

> **Note:** This "dough" is a bit messy to work with in the rolling stage, but once you're past that, these creatures are so cute that you'll never look back.

The SLEEPING BUNNY

MAKES 1 BUNNY

What You'll Need

* Confectioners' sugar
* About 2 tablespoons White Chocolate Dough (see page 117)
* 1 vanilla wafer
* 1 Red Hot

What to Do

1. Put some confectioners' sugar in a small bowl. Line a baking sheet or platter with waxed paper and set aside.

2. For each sleeping bunny:
   - Shape a little less than 2 tablespoons of the dough into a small oval. Make it rounded at one end (the tail) and pointy at the other (the nose).
   - Roll a small ball with the remaining dough to serve as a fluffy tail, and press it into place.

3. Make bunny ears. With a sharp chef's knife, cut a vanilla wafer in half and press both halves into the body, positioning them as seen the photo.

4. To make the nose, push in a Red Hot at the tip of the oval.

5. Use your fingernail to press two eye slits, just behind the Red Hot. Sprinkle the bunny with confectioners' sugar to coat.

6. Chill the finished bunnies on the prepared baking sheet, and then transfer them to a plate for serving.

The OWL

MAKES 1 OWL

What You'll Need

* Confectioners' sugar
* About 2 tablespoons White Chocolate Dough (see page 117)
* 2 chocolate chips
* 1 piece of candy corn, optional

What to Do

1. Put some confectioners' sugar in a small bowl. Line a baking sheet or platter with waxed paper and set aside.

2. For each owl, shape 2 tablespoons of the dough into an elongated oval. Use your fingers to mold the oval into an owl shape, with two pointy ears on top and indentations on each side for the neck. Sit it upright on the waxed paper and press down slightly to flatten the bottom and form a base. Roll the owl in confectioners' sugar to coat.

3. For the eyes, stick two chocolate chips into the face, with the chips' peaks turned inward.

4. For the beak, cut the tip off a piece of candy corn, and push it into the owl's face. If it's not candy-corn season, mold the cookie mixture into a slight point to approximate a beak.

5. To suggest the folds of the wing feathers: with a butter or dinner knife, press a slightly angled line into the owl's breast, curving down the whole front of the body.

6. Chill the finished owls on the prepared baking sheet, and then transfer them to a plate for serving.

The FIELD MOUSE

MAKES 1 MOUSE

What You'll Need

* Confectioners' sugar
* About 2 tablespoons White Chocolate Dough (see page 117)
* Caramel or red licorice string
* 1 round pink candy (such as a Nerd)
* 2 round purple candies (such as Nerds)
* 2 almond slices

What to Do

1. Put some confectioners' sugar in a small bowl. Line a baking sheet or platter with waxed paper and set aside.

2. For each field mouse, shape about 2 tablespoons of the dough into a small oval. As with the bunny (see page 118), make it rounded at one end (the tail) and pointy at the other (the nose). Roll in the confectioners' sugar to coat.

3. For a tail, press a 3" length of caramel string or red licorice into the rounded end.

4. For a nose, press a round pink candy, such as a Nerd, into the pointy tip. Nudge the nose upward, as if the mouse is sniffing.

5. For eyes, press in two purple Nerds.

6. For ears, press the pointed ends of two almond slices into the dough, just above the eyes.

7. Chill the finished mice on the prepared baking sheet, and then transfer them to a plate for serving.

Butterscotch Dough

The butterscotch chips add a potent orangey brown color to the mixture, just right for porcupines and toads.

MAKES ABOUT 2½ CUPS

What You'll Need:

- 24 vanilla wafers
- 6 ounces (1 cup) butterscotch chips
- ¼ cup sour cream

What to Do:

1. Crush the vanilla wafers to crumbs in a food processor. Or you can seal them in a ziplock bag and use a rolling pin to beat and roll them to crumbs.

2. Melt the butterscotch chips by placing them in a medium-size glass bowl and melting in the microwave on high for 1 minute. Whisk well with a fork. If any lumps remain, heat in 10-second blasts, stirring well after each. Be careful not to overheat, or the mixture will scorch or seize.

3. Stir the crumbs into the melted chips, mixing until well combined. Then stir in the sour cream, blending well.

4. Chill the mixture for 15 to 20 minutes, no more, just until it's stiff enough to handle but not too cold. If you leave it in the fridge too long, soften it until workable by giving the mixture short blasts in the microwave, about 20 seconds at a time, stirring well after each.

The PORCUPINE

What You'll Need

* About 2 tablespoons Butterscotch Dough
  (see page 121)
* 1 Red Hot
* Chocolate sprinkles, dragees, or any tiny round
  candy (such as Nerds)
* 5 pretzel sticks

What to Do

1. Line a baking sheet or platter with waxed
   paper and set aside.

2. For each porcupine, shape 2 tablespoons
   of the dough into an oval and place on the
   waxed paper.

3. For the nose, press in a Red Hot.

4. For the eyes, press in two tiny round candies above the nose.

5. For the quills, break five pretzel sticks in
   half and stick the broken ends into the
   back. Porcupines look best when you
   don't add too many quills, so use your
   judgment. Space them out and angle
   them slightly back from the head.

6. Chill the finished porcupines on the prepared baking sheet until firm. Transfer
   them to a platter or plate for serving.

The FROG

What You'll Need

* About ⅓ cup Butterscotch Dough (see page 121)
* Green Dots
* Mini chocolate chips
* Small round green candies (a combination of Nerds and M&Ms works well)
* 2 pretzel sticks
* Green fruit leather

What to Do

1. For each frog, shape about ⅓ cup of the dough into a large rounded disk, a little narrower toward the back half. Lay it on the plate or platter you'll use for serving.

2. For eyes, press mini chocolate chips into the centers of green Dots. Press two Dots into the front of the frog, set wide apart.

3. For the mouth, use the tip of a paring knife to trace a wide smile under the eyes, down low on the edge of the disk. Also use the knife to trace the outline of back legs.

4. Press M&Ms and Nerds on the back to make warts. Stick with the all-green look shown in the photo or be creative with an assortment of colors.

5. To make each webbed foot, break a pretzel stick into three pieces and press the pieces, fanned out, into the dough under one of the back leg outlines. For the webbing, cut a triangle of fruit leather that's wider than the fanned pretzel pieces. Drape it over the pretzels and press down between them. Chill until firm.

HOLIDAY TREATS

6

Holidays almost always mean food. And, more often than not, they include special sweet treats, cookies, and candy. So why not go with the flow and make adorable decorations and great, gooey gifts out of the sweet treats that are inevitably around anyway? Happy building and happy holidays!

EASTER

At Easter, many kids get a basket full of candy, but it's much more fun (and easier on the tooth enamel) to *make* something out of the goods from Peter Cottontail, rather than just snarfing it all. Even before the big day, there are plenty of Easter projects to get everyone in the mood for spring-time treats. Make the sleeping bunnies from the Woodland Animals (see page 118), add innocent candy chicks, and some Fabergé-like chocolate eggs — and the holiday just got that much brighter.

See Sleeping Bunny,
page 118

EASTER CHICKS

What You'll Need

* Shredded sweetened coconut (2–3 tablespoons per chick)
* Green liquid food coloring
* Glazed vanilla doughnut holes (such as Entenmann's Pop'ems)
* Mini chocolate chips or Nerds
* Candy corn
* Candy orange slices

Construction Citations

You can make a little plateful of chicks peeping together on a coconut bed, or sit each one in its own little coconut nest in a cupcake liner. The instructions call for candy orange slices, but if you find the yellow lemon version, so much the chick-ier.

What to Do

1. Put a handful of coconut in a ziplock bag and add a few drops of green food coloring. Seal the bag, then shake and massage the color into the coconut until it is well distributed. Spread the coconut on a plate to dry thoroughly.

2. For each chick:
   - Cut a slice off the base of a doughnut hole so it sits upright.
   - Press two mini chips or purple Nerds into the front for eyes.
   - For the beak, cut the tip off a piece of candy corn and push it into the doughnut gently, just under the eyes.

3. If you're using cupcake papers for nests, put a spoonful of green coconut grass in the bottom and set the chick on top. If you're putting your chicks directly on a platter, spread the green coconut on the platter and nestle your chick(s) down into the grass.

Note: When it comes to adding the green food coloring to the coconut, easy does it, tiger! While I usually extol the virtues of paste colorings and the intense hues they impart, if you want a pale and delicate green for your Easter grass nests, be sure to use liquid coloring and a gentle hand.

4. For wings for each chick, balance a candy orange slice upright on either side of the chick, curve pointing outward, to make little flapping wings. If you like, you can push the bottom edges gently into the sides of the doughnut: the sticky candy and the doughnut's glaze act as just enough glue to keep them together. If you're making a whole plateful of chicks, you may want to turn some of the wings in other directions, to give your plate of chicks a sense of movement.

CANDY-
BEJEWELED EGGS

What You'll Need

* Cream-filled chocolate eggs (such as Cadbury Creme Egg)
* Vanilla Mortar (see page 14) or 1 can store-bought white frosting
* Large chocolate disks (such as Droste) or chocolate squares (such as Ghirardelli), one for each decorated egg
* Sour tape (you can also use gum strips here but sour tape is covered in glistening sugar)
* Mini jelly beans or mini chocolate chips
* Any small round or shiny candy, such as silver and gold dragees or candy pearls

What to Do

1. Unwrap the egg and a chocolate disk or square to serve as the display base. Cover the egg with mortar and perch it on the base, balancing it on the large end.

2. Cut a length of sour tape long enough to go around the egg lengthwise, then use scissors to divide the tape in half all along the length. (You will have two long, narrow lengths of sour tape.) Wrap one around the egg, starting at the base (you can lift it off the chocolate base), following the seam along the side of the egg, ending back under the bottom of the egg. Wrap the other strip the same way, dividing the egg into four lengthwise quarters with the sour tape. Don't worry if you get your fingers in the frosting, you can smooth it out once the egg is back down on its chocolate base.

3. If you like, you can divide the egg again around the middle by wrapping a narrow strip of sour tape around the equator of the egg.

4. Now, decorate! Working within each quarter (or eighth) of the frosted and wrapped egg, press on jelly beans and other candy, making patterns and swirls, just like the jewels on a Fabergé egg. You can make monochromatic eggs with all one color, or make wildly colorful confections of all different sorts. Shiny dragees are particularly jewel-like.

5. For other eggs, vary the type and amount of sour tape used:
   - You might want to skip the horizontal band, or only apply the first sour strip and decorate the egg in two halves.
   - You can also lay the egg on its side on the base and decorate it horizontally, with sour strips across the top half only.

- For some eggs, you could dye the frosting a rich blue or glowing yellow, using paste food coloring.
- Whatever you do, don't skimp on the candy. Every inch of your egg's surface should glow with goodies.

THANKSGIVING

While adults are rushing around making immense amounts of savory food for the huge onslaught of friends and relatives coming for dinner, it's easy for kids to get stranded in front of the TV, watching the Thanksgiving Day parade. With these candy treats to construct, kids can stay busy and participate in the holiday without actually being under your feet in the kitchen — and the results will be something cute enough to decorate the dinner table or anchor the array of desserts.

PILGRIM HATS

What You'll Need

* ✱ 12 fudge-striped shortbread cookies
* ✱ 12 mini peanut butter or caramel cups
* ✱ Chocolate Mortar (see page 14) or 1 can store-bought chocolate frosting
* ✱ Strawberry fruit leather

What to Do

1. To construct the hats, turn the cookies over so the solid chocolate side is on top. Unwrap the miniature cups and use a dab of mortar to glue them, top side down, to the center of the cookie.

2. To make the hatbands, use scissors or a sharp paring knife to cut a strip of the fruit leather about ⅛" wide. Wrap it snugly around the fluted base of the cup, pressing it right up against the cookie. Press the ends together and trim off the excess. The fruit leather is sticky enough that you probably won't need icing to hold the ends together.

3. Cut a square buckle from another piece of fruit leather and press the buckle over the seam in the hatband.

Construction Citations

These funny and cute little candy hats come together with speed and ease, and they're charming on a Thanksgiving dessert table. If you see little hands reaching for them before dinner time, have fun doing your best John Wayne impression and say, "Take it easy there, pilgrim."

ACORNS

MAKES 1 DOZEN ACORNS

What You'll Need

* 6 pieces red, yellow, and orange fruit leather
* Vanilla glazed doughnut holes (such as Entenmann's Pop'ems)
* Chocolate Mortar (see page 15) or 1 can store-bought chocolate frosting
* ¼ cup finely chopped walnuts or pecans
* Licorice or caramel string

What to Do

1. To make the leaves, use scissors to cut out leaf shapes from the fruit leather.
- You can do this freehand by cutting basic ovals with pointed tips, or making a guesstimate at a maple leaf.
- Another option is to pick up fall leaves from your backyard and lay them on top of the fruit leather and cut around them.
- Lay the cut shapes around the outer edge of your serving platter, loosely overlapping them, to serve as the base for your acorns.

2. To make the acorns, cover the top third of each doughnut hole with mortar, and roll the frosted part in the chopped nuts.

3. To make the stems, cut off ¾" pieces of licorice string and poke them into the mortar on top of each doughnut-hole acorn. (Don't worry about penetrating the doughnut.)

4. Mound the completed acorns atop the fruit-leather leaves.

Construction Citations

You can make a mound of very cute acorn doughnut holes in a hurry. Arrange them on a platter on top of leaves snipped from red, orange, and yellow fruit leather, and you have a Thanksgiving centerpiece any child will love.

TURKEYS

What You'll Need

* Nutter Butter cookies
* Vanilla Mortar (see page 15) or 1 can store-bought chocolate frosting
* Mini marshmallows
* Mini chocolate chips
* Candy corn
* Red fruit leather or red decorating gel
* Fudge-striped shortbread cookies (two for each turkey)

Construction Citations

On the holiday, young hands can stay occupied with this project — and the resulting turkeys make great place-card holders! Just tuck a little card, with each diner's name, behind the turkey's head. (Don't do it too many hours before dinner is served, or grease will leach onto the paper!)

What to Do

1. For each turkey, lay a Nutter Butter flat on your work surface. For the eyes, put two dabs of mortar on one end of the cookie and press two mini chocolate chips into the wet frosting. For the beak, trim off the tip of a candy corn and mortar it in place. Cut a little strip of red fruit leather and glue it alongside the beak, letting it dangle down beneath to serve as the wattle. If you don't have fruit leather, you can use a squeeze of red decorating gel.

2. With mortar, glue the back of the Nutter Butter to the front of a fudge-striped shortbread cookie. Use more mortar to glue candy corn to the back of the striped cookie. Place the candy corn so that the fat ends radiate outward.

> **Fun Variation:** These goofy turkeys are even cuter if you have the brown "Indian corn" candy corn (with brown ends instead of yellow), which is sometimes available in late fall. (If you see it, stock up!) Or be sure to save some regular candy corn from Halloween, because Thanksgiving will be here before you know it.

3. With a thick dollop of frosting, glue the Nutter Butter and fudge-striped cookie in a standing position on a second fudge-striped cookie that is lying flat. It helps to sort of nestle the rounded base of the Nutter Butter into the hole in the middle of the shortbread cookie.

Blueprints

This is one project where using a few dabs of peanut butter in place of frosting is fast, easy, entirely appropriate, and even totally tasty. Be sure to use creamy peanut butter, not crunchy. Also, do *not* use the natural kind, which is less sticky because it's grainier and oilier, lacking the sugar and emulsifiers that smooth out other types of peanut butter.

CHRISTMAS

Christmas tends to be accompanied by so much candy and so many baked goods, it's hard to imagine you need an excuse for *more*. But these easy-to-make little goodies let kids be an active part of the holiday season instead of passively partaking of the endless supply of sweets. The candy Christmas trees, wrapped in cellophane, can serve as gifts for young friends or even be tied to a present. The snowmen are both a perfect kiddie activity and a tasty treat for a holiday party. The sleigh, replete with a chocolate Santa, is a fun table decoration — and don't forget to surround St. Nick with a forest of candy Christmas trees!

CHRISTMAS TREES

What You'll Need

* Rice Krispies Treats (see page 17) with green paste coloring added to the melted marshmallow before stirring in the cereal
* Small colorful candies such as Red Hots, Dots, M&Ms Minis, and mini gumdrops
* Silver and gold dragees and/or pearlized dragees
* 1 cup white chocolate chips, optional
* Multicolored mini marshmallows or red or green holiday M&Ms, optional

What to Do

1. Line a large baking sheet with waxed paper before starting work, and put out a small dish of butter or vegetable oil for greasing your hands. Grease a platter generously and pour the warm Rice Krispies Treats onto the platter.

2. To form the trees:
   - As soon as the treats are cool enough to handle, grease your hands and scoop up about ½ cup of the mixture. Working quickly, shape it into a cone about 4" high.
   - Set each cone on the waxed-paper-lined baking sheet and continue, working quickly so the mixture doesn't stiffen up before you finish shaping all the trees.
   - If the mixture does get stiff, you can reheat it in the microwave for 45 seconds and see if it has softened enough to continue. Don't overheat, or the mixture may scorch.

Note: If you're doing this project with a group of kids, shape the trees first yourself and let the kids do all the decorating with the candy and chocolate.

3. While the trees are still warm, press in candies as ornaments. You can make bright, multicolored trees, and also make

a few stylishly monochromatic trees, such as all gold or all silver dragees.

4. If you like, you can drizzle on snow. Put the white chocolate chips in a small bowl and microwave on high for 1 minute, no longer. Whisk the chips vigorously with a fork. While they may appear solid when you take them out of the microwave, they'll soften and melt right away when you whisk. If there are any remaining lumps, you can wait a minute or two and whisk again, or microwave again in 10-second bursts, no longer, whisking after each. Overheating the chocolate will make it scorch or seize into a stiff mass.

> **Easy Variation:** If you don't like the idea of kids tossing around melted chocolate with a fork, use store-bought tubes of white icing or confectioners' sugar (as shown in the photographs) instead.

5. Use a fork to drizzle the melted white chocolate over each tree. The best way to achieve thin lines is to hold the fork high above the trees and let the chocolate drip down from on high. If you find the size of your baking sheet constraining, you can spread a few sheets of waxed paper directly on your table or work surface and space the trees out. Then hold the bowl up high with the fork, so you dip and drip without reaching down each time.

6. Let the trees firm up at room temperature. If the room is very warm, you may want to put them in the fridge or freezer for a few moments to set the chocolate, but don't store them that way or the humidity will soften up the Rice Krispies mixture.

Blueprints

You're not likely to find them in just any old store, but it *is* possible to buy gummy stars that are the perfect size for topping your candy Christmas trees. If you can find them (or you can order them on the Internet), wait until you've finished decorating the trees and they have cooled and started to firm up. Then top them with a gummy star, gluing it on with a bit of the melted white chocolate. If you can't find any star-shaped candy to top your tree, trim multicolored mini-marshmallows into tiny stars with a pair of pointy scissors, or use the white chocolate to glue a red or green holiday M&M upright on top.

▼▼▼▼▼▼▼▼▼▼
ℰSNOWMEN

see photo page 137

What You'll Need

* Pretzel sticks
* Powdered-sugar doughnut holes
* Powdered-sugar mini doughnuts
* Mini chocolate chips
* Candy corn
* Red decorating gel
* Fruit leather
* Chocolate disks (such as Droste)
* Mini caramel or peanut-butter cups
* Small dollop of mortar or peanut butter, optional

What to Do

1. To make the basic snowmen:
   - Push a pretzel stick halfway into a doughnut hole, then push the other end into a second doughnut hole. Push the doughnut holes together until you can't see the pretzel stick.
   - Balance these two stacked doughnut holes on top of a mini doughnut. You can also balance a single doughnut hole on a mini doughnut for a short snowman, or stack three doughnut holes with pretzel supports, cutting a slice off the bottom so the snowman sits flat.

2. To decorate the snowmen, press mini chips up the front for buttons, and press two chips into the top doughnut hole for eyes. If you like your buttons smaller, cut the mini chips into quarters and use those pieces instead of whole chips.

3. To make a nose, cut the pointy end off a piece of candy corn and press this tiny tip into the middle of the snowman's face.

4. Pipe on a smile with red decorating gel, or cut a few more mini chips into quarters and poke the pieces into the doughnut in a smile shape.

5. To make the scarf, cut a long rectangular slice from fruit leather with scissors, and snip a little fringe at each end. Tie it around the snowman's neck.

6. For the hat, cut a very small slice off the top of the snowman's head (to make a flat place for the hat to sit), then put a chocolate disk on his head. Top it with an upside-down caramel mini cup or mini peanut butter cup. If the hat feels too precarious, use frosting or peanut butter to stick it down. With the red decorating gel, pipe a hatband around the base of the mini cup.

SANTA'S SLEIGH

MAKES 1 SLEIGH

What You'll Need

* 3 (1.55-ounce) white chocolate bars, such as Hershey's Cookies and Cream (the kind that is evenly divided into rectangles)
* Vanilla Mortar (see page 14) or 1 can store-bought vanilla frosting
* Medium candy canes (the kind with curved ends)

* Small colorful candies such as Nerds, gumballs, Red Hots, M&Ms Minis, and seasonal candies
* Royal Icing Glue (see page 16) or white decorating gel
* Starburst fruit chews
* 1 foil-wrapped decorated chocolate Santa
* Small chocolates wrapped like gifts, optional

What to Do

1. To make the sleigh, lay down one whole chocolate bar to serve as the sleigh's base. With frosting, glue one set of eight attached pieces (four pieces over four pieces) along the back edge of the sleigh's base, then glue a strip of four attached pieces on either side to serve as the sleigh's sides, forming a 3-sided box that's open in the front and higher in the back.

2. To make runners for the sleigh, turn the curved ends of the candy canes upward and spread a little mortar along the top of each cane. Position the canes beneath or alongside the sleigh, at the outer edges.

3. Spread a line of mortar along the side and back edges of the sleigh. Stick Nerds, gumdrops, or other small candies into the mortar to decorate the sleigh as you like.

4. To make Santa's gifts, unwrap several fruit chews. Pour the royal icing into a small ziplock bag and cut off the very tip of one corner, so you can squeeze out a narrow line of icing. Squeeze a white ribbon of frosting onto the fruit chews, crisscrossing the top of each one, then pipe out a little bow in the center. Stack the fruit-chew gifts in the bottom of the sleigh.

Easy Variation: Fill your sleigh with small chocolates wrapped to look like gifts, as in the photograph on page 141, or any other candy that Santa might have in his bag.

5. Stand a chocolate Santa beside the gifts for some delicious Christmas cheer!

CANDY CONSTRUCTION NOTES

In the set designs for this book, we used a lot of edibles to create environments for the projects. If you want to makes whole scenes for your creations too, here are some ideas.

CANDY CONSTRUCTION SITE

Dirt — graham cracker crumbs, crushed pretzels, and grated unsweetened baking chocolate; *Caution cones* — candy corn; *Rock pile* — rock candy; *Dirt pile* — raw sugar

FUDGE BROWNIE STEAM TRAIN

Grass — coconut tinted with green food coloring; *Track* — black licorice rails and licorice string ties; *Dirt* — see Candy Construction Site; *Trees* — spice drops and Dots for foliage and licorice for trunks; *Rocks* — candy pebbles

RACE CARS

Track — black sanding sugar; *Grass* — coconut tinted with green food coloring; *Pit crew* — Starburst for bodies, licorice for arms, legs, and feet, and Whoppers for heads and helmets; *Pennants* — fruit leather and string licorice

BIPLANE AND HELICOPTER

It could be fun to set these on clouds of cotton candy.

OUTER SPACE

Planet — Hershey's Kisses on foil-wrapped styrofoam sphere; *Stars* — foil-wrapped chocolate stars

PYRAMIDS OF GIZA

Sand — table sugar tinted with food coloring; *Sun* — Fruit Roll-Ups

PIRATE SHIP

Ocean — jelly beans, M&Ms, and blue Twizzlers, with rock candy for breakers; *Beach* — chocolate coins; *Fish* — gummy sharks and Swedish fish

MARTIAN-MALLOWS AND ALIENS

Platforms — whirly pops

FAIRY-TALE CASTLE

King and queen — fruit leather for capes, spice drops and Starlights for bodies, Whoppers for heads, and gem candies for crowns; *Grass* — coconut tinted with green food coloring and Nerds for scattered flowers; *Moat* — fruit leather for water and white-chocolate-covered almonds for stone border; *Alligator* — gummy candy, black licorice, and white Nerds; *Path (white castle)* — sugar pearls sprinkles; *Path (pink castle)*— mini Jawbreakers; *Trees (pink castle)* — Dum Dums; *Pennants* — fruit leather; *Torches* — Lambertz Zimsterne cookies and Twizzlers

BOARD GAMES

Parquet — graham crackers

CANDY SUSHI

Chopsticks — Pixie Stix; *Chopstick rest* — marshmallow half

CREEPY-CRAWLIES

Grass — coconut tinted with green food coloring; *Flowers* — Starlights and fruit leather

WOODLAND CREATURES

Large mushrooms — spice drops and Nerds for caps and Twizzlers for stems; *Small mushrooms* — Dots for caps and white dough for stems; *Tree trunks* — Oreo Fun Stix, Pepperidge Farm Pirouettes, and chocolate-covered pretzel rods; *Dirt* — graham cracker crumbs, Anna's chocolate mint cookies, and dark chocolate shavings; *Rocks* — candy pebbles

EASTER

Sanding sugar

THANKSGIVING

Assorted nuts

CHRISTMAS

White table sugar or coconut could be used for a dusting of snow.

Other Storey Titles You Will Enjoy

250 Treasured Country Desserts, by Andrea Chesman & Fran Raboff.
A nostalgic collection of more than 250 recipes for home bakers to rely on
for all occasions.
416 pages. Paper. ISBN 978-1-60342-152-2.

The Baking Answer Book, by Lauren Chattman.
Answers every question about common and specialty ingredients, the best
equipment, and the science behind the magic of baking.
384 pages. Flexibind. ISBN 978-1-60342-439-4.

Cookie Craft, by Valerie Peterson & Janice Fryer.
Clear instruction, practical methods, and all the tips and tricks for beautifully
decorated special occasion cookies.
168 pages. Hardcover. ISBN 978-1-58017-694-1.

Cookie Craft Christmas, by Valerie Peterson & Janice Fryer.
Fresh inspiration and fabulous decorating from authors of Cookie Craft, with
more than 60 new designs for Christmas cookies.
176 pages. Hardcover with jacket. ISBN 978-1-60342-440-0.

Ghoulish Goodies, by Sharon Bowers.
A colorful collection of creepy treats for celebrating Halloween or any
frightful occasion.
160 pages. Paper. ISBN 978-1-60342-146-1.

These and other books from Storey Publishing are available
wherever quality books are sold or by calling 1-800-441-5700.
Visit us at *www.storey.com*.